God Doesn't Make Mistakes

Praise for God Doesn't Make Mistakes

Leslie pours her heart and soul into each chapter of her amazing new book! *God Doesn't Make Mistakes* is the perfect combination of realism, humor, and religion. She gives a practical overview of how one individual not only faces life's challenges but solves them using Biblical principles. Prepare to be challenged and empowered!

—*DL Wallace, Founder and CEO, Success Training Institute*

This book is amazing! It's inspiring, introspective, and thought provoking. It's like having a conversation with yourself, your best friend (Leslie), and Jesus at the same time. It makes you feel safe (with your thoughts and feelings) and challenges you at the same time—how did you do that? It is what every woman needs as she enters, leaves, or is in the midst of the storm. Kudos, girl! You let God use you and I thank you!

—*Sharnikya Howard, Founder, Life Abundantly Coaching*

The level of transparency penned by Leslie in *God Doesn't Make Mistakes* is powerful on many levels. The authenticity and vulnerability in her shared journal entries as well as the reflections as she journeyed through many internal and external battles released a healing power, encouragement, and hope. As I read the book, her growth in discerning the voice of ABBA, receiving what He revealed in each situation and applying it to her life, was convicting, liberating, and affirming all at the same time. Get ready to be filled with hope, joy, and many new perspectives throughout the book as Leslie takes you on a "behind the scenes" journey of her most intimate thoughts . . . from her heart to Abba Father's heart and vice versa. As you take this journey through these pages, you too should pen those life experiences and emotions that flash into your thoughts. Thank you, Leslie, for your HEART work. Your "YES" has and will continue to bless and shift many Souls.

—*Dr. J. Le'Ray, Founder and CEO, Heart 2 Heart Services*

God Doesn't Make Mistakes

Learning How Our Missteps Fit Into His Perfect Plan

LESLIE R. GREEN

GOD DOESN'T MAKE MISTAKES
Published by Purposely Created Publishing Group™
Copyright © 2019 Leslie R. Green

All rights reserved.

No part of this book may be reproduced, distributed or transmitted in any form by any means, graphic, electronic, or mechanical, including photocopy, recording, taping, or by any information storage or retrieval system, without permission in writing from the publisher, except in the case of reprints in the context of reviews, quotes, or references.

Printed in the United States of America

ISBN: 978-1-949134-73-5

Special discounts are available on bulk quantity purchases by book clubs, associations and special interest groups. For details email: sales@publishyourgift.com or call (888) 949-6228.

For information logon to:
www.PublishYourGift.com

I dedicate this book to my dad, who always reminded me to "work hard, have fun, and never lose your sense of humor." I miss you Daddy, and I'll love you always and forever.

Table of Contents

Foreword by Keith A. Battle 1

Introduction 3

THE BIG PICTURE
(November 9, 2015) 7

THE WAIT
(November 16, 2015) 19

FREE WILL
(December 1, 2015) 31

SPIRITUAL WARFARE
(December 3, 2015) 45

PURPOSE
(December 7, 2015) 61

GRATEFULNESS
(December 17, 2015) 73

MY LIFE IS A PRAISE SONG
(December 20, 2015) 85

GOD'S WILL BE DONE
(December 23, 2015) 99

GOD'S DELAYS ARE NOT ALWAYS HIS DENIALS
(December 30, 2015) 111

FORGIVENESS
(January 11, 2016) 123

BONUS CHAPTER
My Sleeping Adam 131

Conclusion 137

References 141

About the Author 143

Foreword

As the senior pastor of Zion Church, chaplain of the Washington Wizards, and an author, speaker, and entrepreneur, I am always looking for ways to grow so that I can better serve the people that I've been blessed to serve. And one of the most important tools that I've used to help me grow, especially throughout the course of my adult life, has been a journal. I have journaled my prayers, my fears, my failures, my hopes, my dreams, and even my secrets for years, and it's one of the most precious gifts that I have. Being able to chronicle your own life's story is a powerful mechanism, especially when you take some time to reflect back on your journey and see the patterns and lessons that are threaded through the tapestry of your life.

In this book, *God Doesn't Make Mistakes*, Leslie Green uses her own personal journal not only to help shape and craft the book, but also to transparently share some of her deepest struggles and greatest life-lessons learned. She opens up her personal life and shares both her victories and her defeats.

In addition, this heartfelt work by Leslie is not only filled with the authenticity of her personal story; the book is also absolutely brimming with helpful biblical references. These make it perfect to use as a devotional book, one to enjoy in the morning with a cup of coffee to help prepare for your day. Or, it can serve as a great reflective read while you're on exercise equipment getting in your workout at the gym.

And what's also cool about the book is the fact that in spite of her spiritual and professional success, Leslie doesn't talk to you as if she's the expert and her readers are all students. Instead, she talks and walks with you on a faith journey that trusts that God is always lovingly working out His wonderful plan for our lives, even when we make mistakes.

Be prepared to see your faith grow and your commitment to God be strengthened as you read this wonderful book.

Peace & blessings,
Keith A. Battle

Introduction

Typically, on the days leading into a new year, I believe most people are hopeful and optimistic about what that new year will bring. They are thinking about the goals they are going to accomplish, bad habits they are going to break finally, and milestone events that are set to take place. Typically, I'm one of those people. However, on the eve of 2015, I had an entirely different experience. I was nervous, uneasy, and uncharacteristically sad. Yes, Miss #IamGoldenLife herself was in the dumps. In hindsight, my efforts to force myself to be optimistic about the coming year were futile because subconsciously I was anticipating what would be one of the most challenging years of my life. Yet I still wasn't mentally, emotionally, or spiritually prepared for the turn of events that would follow.

The details of what happened aren't really important right now, but there were three major life events that took place all within the span of the first two weeks of the year. My relationship of nearly five years, that I had thought was headed toward marriage, abruptly came to an end. A new boss was forced upon me, one who came complete with a new set of rules, lowered office morale, and an increased workload, which was already filled to the brim. And, for the finale, I landed in the hospital with pneumonia. Mind, body, and spirit, I thought I was being attacked. And by some definitions you might say I was.

Externally the days, weeks, and months that followed must have looked pretty normal, if not grand, to others on the outside looking in, even to those pretty close to me. But internally, I was being broken down, stirred up, and twisted around. All of a sudden, everything I was so certain about was seemingly a complete fluke. On top of that, I felt like I had lost my sense of purpose. (In reality, I hadn't even begun to find it.) While my body had healed from the pneumonia, my mental, emotional, and spiritual healing would take much longer to transpire.

By June, I had resigned from my job, become a full-time entrepreneur, and launched a whole new division of my company, Golden Life Ventures, that I had until then been operating on a part-time basis. That was a major transition in itself. I managed to convince myself that, despite how the year began, 2015 was going to be my best year yet. I spoke it, but God and I disagreed on what that looked like.

In November, another pivotal moment took place for me. After attempting to jump back into the dating scene prematurely (as I now believe in hindsight) and failing at it miserably, I decided one night to start reading through my journals, as far back as seven years prior. I was really searching for a pattern or some type of explanation of how I had gotten to the undesired place in which I found myself. The epiphanies that began to pour out from that process were staggering. I began to see, there in my own words, the consequences—and blessings for that matter, which I'll get to in a minute—of my disobedience. I witnessed how God would give me direction via my prayers and thought processes and then I would turn right around and go the opposite way. The consequences of those actions were, in many cases, that I got the opposite results of what I really wanted. But the blessings of those actions were that I learned something from them, and in some cases, when tested in that area again, I passed; and even better, a testimony came out of it that blessed someone else. Won't He do it!

What I learned at the conclusion of that journal review process was the genesis of this book. God doesn't make mistakes; people do. The good news about the mistakes we make is that there are no mistakes we can make that can change God's perfect plan for us. In fact, God is so amazing, He's already factored our mistakes and those of others into His divine will for our lives!

This book gives you an inside peek into several journal entries I wrote during the latter part of what was one of the most challenging, yet transformational, seasons of my life. Come with me on a journey of discovery about how God has woven our mistakes into His perfect tapestry, and how

His BEST plans come as a result of our obedience, trust, and faithfulness.

> All things are done according to God's plan and decision; and God chose us to be his own people in union with Christ because of his own purpose, based on what he had decided from the very beginning.
>
> —Ephesians 1:11 (GNT)

the Big picture

Yet God has made everything beautiful for its own time. He has planted eternity in the human heart, but even so, people cannot see the whole scope of God's work from beginning to end.

—Ecclesiastes 3:11 (NLT)

Journal Entry (November 9, 2015):

Pastor Larry Paige preached a sermon yesterday about The Big Picture that felt like it was directly aimed at me. Over the last few days as I've been going back through my journal entries as far back as 2008, it has given me a lot of perspective. It's amazing what hindsight can do for your perspective. And even though I still don't know the whole picture, I can see where God was moving in my life and I was resisting Him the whole way because I had my own plans in mind.

I wrote down a quote from one of my favorite TV shows, <u>Being Mary Jane</u>, the other day... "We have to let go of the life we planned to accept the one that is waiting for us." That is me! Me and my plans, ugh. It's really the only reason I ever get disappointed. I have much for which to be grateful, but because I'm not getting what I want when I want it, I feel a certain type of way. I know my situation is not unique, but it feels personal because it happens to me. And I've lived a pretty charmed life. I don't truly know what it feels like to be broke and lonely. It's all relative. I only feel this way because I knew what it felt like to be making over $100K/year and I had someone special in my life for over four years. I need to get over myself.

Pastor Paige said, "... our problems are as big as we make them, because at the end of the day, none of our problems are bigger than God. He's the one orchestrating everything." He's got plans for me and He knows exactly where I'm going. There's no mistake I can make that will keep me from getting there. It may delay it, but I'll still get there. That's a refreshing thought. My job is to just be patient and trust Him. I don't know how many times I'll have to hear that before it finally sinks in. Perhaps today I've finally learned that lesson.

Our Plans

> Look here, you who say, "Today or tomorrow we are going to a certain town and will stay there a year. We will do business there and make a profit." How do you know what your life will be like tomorrow? Your life is like the morning fog—it's here a little while, then it's gone. What you ought to say is, "If the Lord wants us to, we will live and do this or that." Otherwise you are boasting about your own pretentious plans, and all such boasting is evil.
>
> —James 4:13 (NLT)

My whole life I've been a planner. You could say I got it from my momma. We like to plan things out so we'll have the best experience possible. Sounds reasonable, right? For many things in life that works, and there's nothing wrong with wanting to be prepared, right? When it comes to planning out one's life, however, that can be a little tricky . . . especially when you try to do that as a twelve-year-old.

Like many little girls, when I was younger I started to form plans for my life based on what I saw adults around me do, particularly my parents. I didn't quite know what my career was going to be, because at the time I had many interests and talents. But I did know that I would be established in whatever career of my choice by the time I was twenty-five, married by twenty-six or twenty-seven, have a few years with my husband, and then begin to have our children, a boy and a girl, just like my mom and dad.

Before you judge me, think back to when you were a kid and what your vision or plan for your life looked like. Perhaps for you, it was not doing what your parents did; maybe it was doing the exact opposite of what they did. And maybe you weren't twelve, you were sixteen when you made those plans. Whatever the case may be, we've all been there at a young age. Then as we began to grow older, we realized there were a whole lot of things over which we had no control that could come into play and blow that whole plan to hell.

I don't know at what moment I discovered that fact; perhaps it was a gradual enlightenment process that happened. Despite that discovery, I still went into my adult life believing that, even as a saved Christian woman, it was okay to go full steam ahead with my plans without consulting God FIRST. Actually, I consulted God a lot, but it was rarely first. And when I did consult Him, it was a quick prayer, and without waiting and listening for an answer, I went ahead and moved forward with MY plans. In some cases, I got exactly what I planned for—and later realized I really didn't want what I had thought I wanted. In other scenarios, I failed at making my plans come to fruition, and found that what I got as a result of that failure was much better than the thing I wanted anyway.

That's called God's grace and mercy. The way I've heard it described is that grace is getting what you don't deserve, while mercy is not getting what you do deserve. One thing is certain: while I was busy going after my plans, inside or outside of His will, He was teaching me valuable lessons along the way that I believe now ultimately fit into the bigger picture of His plan for me.

> We can make our plans, but the Lord determines our steps.
>
> —Proverbs 16:9 (NLT)

Because God has granted us an unlimited amount of His grace and mercy, we must be careful not to abuse it. Sometimes I believe we treat our grace as a permission slip to get by. Here is a lesson I had to learn the hard way: Just because you haven't gotten caught, or you don't wear your sins publicly, does not mean God is okay with you living in sin, because in the end, "God knows my heart." His grace and mercy are gifts and we should treat them as such. It's one thing to make a mistake; it's an entirely different thing to knowingly live a lifestyle of sin and disobedience and yet expect God's grace to cover it all.

Our Mistakes

> If we claim we have no sin, we are only fooling ourselves and not living in the truth.
>
> —1 John 1:8 (NLT)

There is a reason God did not make us perfect. While He made us in His own image, He did not make us His equals.

We are wonderfully flawed so that we can depend on Him and understand our place in reverent fear of Him. Because we are flawed, it's natural for us to make mistakes . . . a lot of them. It doesn't feel good when it happens, especially when there are brutal consequences, but it's important for us to know that even our mistakes can be used for our good. In fact, making mistakes is oftentimes the best way we learn and develop discernment. Think about that first—and likely only—time you touched a hot stove or iron on purpose. Discernment developed through pain and disappointment teaches you how to make better decisions in the future.

And here's something that blew me away and freed me, once I really got it: God's providence is so amazing, He has already perfectly factored our errors into His future plans for us.

Does this mean we shouldn't be careful, and should just live life haphazardly, expecting God to clean up our mess? Absolutely not. As I said before, ultimately, He wants us to live a life that is pleasing to Him and be obedient. That is an act of worship and love on our part, and the good news is, God has given us a roadmap to follow in the Bible through the life of Jesus Christ.

> But those who obey God's word truly show how completely they love him. That is how we know we are living in him. Those who say they live in God should live their lives as Jesus did.
>
> —1 John 2:5–6 (NLT)

When we do mess up and make mistakes, He wants us to rely on Him for His divine guidance and wisdom to move forward. One thing is for sure, He is always with us and He has given us permission to call on Him for help. That is a huge comfort!

The bottom line is, life is meant to be lived in collaboration with God. We should not make decisions and ask God to bless them afterward. He wants us to be still long enough to listen to Him, and we'll find that the decisions we make together, based on our obedience, have much better outcomes.

He says, "Be still and know that I am God."

—Psalm 46:10a (NIV)

Our Obedience

Remember, it is sin to know what you ought to do and then not do it.

—James 4:17 (NLT)

From an early age I was led to church. My family did not have a church home growing up, so we only went to church on special occasions (weddings, funerals, baptisms, etc.) or at random when someone invited us to their church.

Upon an invitation from a friend to attend her church, I began to regularly attend, even without my family, and eventually joined the church and immersed myself in several ministries. I was twelve. If you asked me then what it was that led me to do all of that at such a young age without my family (although they were supportive), I would say "something just led me." As I got older, I described it like many people do, as "my gut" told me. Into my adulthood, as I've grown more spiritually, I've come to the revelation that all along, it was my conviction. My understanding of *conviction* is that it is God's voice speaking from within, or in other words, it is the Holy Spirit leading. When I think back to when I've ignored that conviction, many times I eventually suffered some sort of consequence from that disobedience. Conversely, when I listened to it and obeyed, I was saved from something bad happening. Sometimes nothing happens . . . or so I thought. Honestly, though, there are probably a number of outcomes where that voice saved me that I'll never know.

I share that because I've heard people, mostly self-professed Christians, ask the question, "How do I know if God is speaking to me?" Or, diving even deeper, "How do I even know if I'm being obedient versus disobedient if I can't hear God telling me what to do or not to do?" I believe that if you have any type of relationship with Him, you will know and it will be clear when God is speaking to you, especially when you ask Him to speak and make it clear. If you've ever had some type of conviction, that is one of the ways God speaks to you. You can call it your gut or a tiny little voice in your head, but consider the idea that the voice you're hearing is His. And that's just one of the many ways He speaks.

> I will pursue your commands, for you expand my understanding. Teach me your decrees, O Lord; I will keep them to the end. Give me understanding and I will obey your instructions; I will put them into practice with all my heart. Make me walk along the path of your commands, for that is where my happiness is found.
>
> —Psalm 119:32–35 (NLT)

Once you become aware of and can discern how and when God speaks to you, it's a conscious decision to be disobedient if you choose not to follow what that voice is telling you to do. The problem is, oftentimes our flesh tells us one thing and the Holy Spirit tells us another, and unfortunately, the flesh has its way more often than not if we don't recognize what's happening. We are naturally sinful beings, so that's why we have to do everything in our power to get and stay close to Him, so that the flesh doesn't have a fighting chance. One way to stay close to Him and know Him intimately is through reading His word.

> But don't just listen to God's word. You must do what it says. Otherwise, you are only fooling yourselves. For if you listen to the word and don't obey, it is like glancing at your face in the mirror. You see yourself, walk away, and forget what you look like. But if you look carefully into the perfect law that sets you free, and if you do what it says and don't forget what you heard, then God will bless you for doing it.
>
> —James 1:22–25 (NLT)

One of the benefits of journaling is that, if you are really honest with yourself as you write, you get to dump all of your thoughts and feelings onto paper, and then reflect back on them later after you've lived through them. I wrote about red flags that the Holy Spirit was waving in my face and what I knew I should do versus what I actually did. In hindsight, I can see where my disobedience caused me problems because my faith wasn't yet strong enough to trust that God would cover me. Because I couldn't see the bigger picture and I was letting my emotions, feelings, flesh, and limited understanding lead me, I thought that my way was the right way. God told me the way I should go, at times very subtly and sometimes very loudly, but many times I didn't listen because I was anxious to get to the place where I wanted to go.

One lesson of many that I learned in the end was the value of not just listening for God's voice, but of waiting for His voice. He doesn't always speak right away. I believe He makes us wait on hearing His voice on purpose, so we can build that muscle of trusting Him in the silence.

> Let all that I am wait quietly before God, for my hope is in him.
>
> —Psalm 62:5 (NLT)

REFLECTIONS

REFLECTIONS

the Wait

Journal Entry (November 16, 2015)

This morning's devotional talked about our tendency as humans to look at our day, week, month ahead and become overwhelmed/intimidated by all of the "stuff" that awaits us. But once we remember The One who is with us always, holding us by the hand, we begin to relax in His presence because a peaceful fog has obscured the view of all that lies ahead. We can see only a few steps ahead of us, so we turn our attention to Him, the one who guides us.

But we/I don't always do that, do I? I get frustrated at the fog. I want it to move so I can see. Sometimes I actually convince myself that if I can just see around the corner, I'll be good. I'll be at peace. That's not the case though. Perhaps I can't see around the corner because I'm not ready or prepared for what is there. There is protection in that obscured view. I think I'm ready for what God has planned, but the reality is I'm not. If I were, He would allow me to see/have/go through it.

Just when I think I've learned patience, I'm called to wait a little while longer. God doesn't want me to be frustrated. He wants me to be at peace. I need to find out how to do a better job of accessing His peace while I wait . . . and for that matter, His joy as well. I get small doses of it, but I want to have access to joy ALL the time. The truth is, I do have access to it all the time. I'm just not good at tapping into that access. I believe that I'm getting better though. I've acknowledged it's a problem. That's the first step.

Patience

> But if we hope for what we do not see, we wait for it with patience.
>
> —Romans 8:25 (ESV)

I remember I used to pray for patience all the time. Then I kept getting into situations that required me to wait, so I stopped praying for it. Be careful what you ask for, right? But that's how God works. When you ask for something, He gives you opportunities to use or exercise what He's given you, otherwise known as tests. I hate tests. I actually don't know anyone who likes them. (I take that back. There was this girl in my class all through elementary school who absolutely loved tests, and she got on my nerves. But I digress.)

We have to be careful with how we understand that word, *test*. Sometimes we operate as if we believe that God is purposefully setting out to hurt us or harm us, or even to let bad things happen to us in order to teach us a lesson. That couldn't be further from the truth. If we view God's tests in the way we viewed tests or exams in school, we would understand that tests are not punishment (though sometimes they seemed like they were). Tests are actually meant to evaluate how well you've learned a lesson. If you pass a test, you can move on and perhaps get promoted. If you fail, however, it's just an indication that you have more to learn. Perhaps when God "tests" us, He's giving us an opportunity to either get promoted or review a lesson we really need to get right.

For me, the lesson was/is patience. Patience is one thing I've struggled with my whole life. I was born a few weeks before my due date. I took my first steps at ten months old, even before I crawled. I joke with my mom that it was because I had someplace to be! I want things to happen the way I've planned and I want them to happen RIGHT NOW! Judge me all you want, but I know I'm not alone in this. There came a time, though, when I had to realize and accept the fact that when I'm not being patient, I'm actually being disobedient to the Lord's will for my life.

> Wait patiently for the Lord. Be brave and courageous. Yes, wait patiently for the Lord.
>
> —Psalm 27:14 (NLT)

That devotional I was referring to in this journal entry challenged me because it showed me that sometimes God calls me to wait not because He doesn't want me to have what I desire, but because I'm not quite ready yet for what He wants me to have. I have to learn some things first, and learning lessons can't be rushed. God doesn't want me to fail, and I'm certain He doesn't want you to fail either.

This learning process also revealed that waiting is purposeful because God wants to show us how to wait. Our "how" reveals the level of trust we have in Him. In both of the verses from Psalms about waiting that are quoted in this chapter, the word "patiently" follows "wait." He doesn't just want us to wait, biting our nails, throwing temper tantrums, or having mini-panic attacks (or maybe that's just me). He wants us to wait patiently. And we should trust and believe that His promise always follows.

> And so after waiting patiently, Abraham received what was promised.
>
> —Hebrews 6:15 (NIV)

The other thing I started praying for, upon my pastor's influence, was for God to show me *me*. That was a scary process. I was basically asking Him to test me, and *that* He did! If I had known then what I know now about how that answered prayer would turn out, I wonder if I would have been courageous enough to ask that prayer again. That's where that fog comes in that I mentioned in my journal entry. I honestly didn't know what I was asking when I uttered those words, "Show me *me*." It was an invitation for more tests—and you know how I feel about those. Looking back, the year of 2015, and most of the year that followed, was nothing but one big test. Little did I know it came from that one simple, answered prayer.

> Search me, O God, and know my heart; test me and know my anxious thoughts. Point out anything in me that offends you, and lead me along the path of everlasting life.
>
> —Psalm 139:23–24 (NLT)

... *Show me* me ...

Courage

While I was going through that challenging season, Psalm 27:14 kept coming up for me. It was like that car you just bought that now, miraculously, you see everyone else driving. The scripture had always been there, but never spoke to me like it did in that season. It kept coming up because God really wanted me to hear Him say, "Be patient and be still in this season, because I want to show you some things." One of the crucial things He taught me was that waiting takes courage. It takes courage to see people all around you getting what they want, and even what you want, while you sit still in your season of waiting. It takes courage to submit to God's timing when you want to go full speed ahead with something that you believe, with your limited understanding, is right.

Jesus told us the life of a Christ follower would not be easy. We may think He was just talking about those who lived in biblical times, but no; He's talking about us in the twenty-first century, too, and those who will live after us as well. We fight different battles than those that Christ followers of biblical times fought, and some would argue, myself included, that those disciples had it far worse, because they were faced with physical persecution and death for following Christ. Our battles are mostly with worldly ideologies and cultural and social norms that are strikingly at odds against pretty much everything Jesus Christ stood for and taught.

I cannot talk about this subject of having the courage to wait without getting into a consistent struggle throughout my spiritual walk with sexual purity and abstinence before marriage. I probably don't have to tell you that waiting for sex until marriage is not a normal thing to do in the society or culture in which we live. Very few people close to me (I can count them on one hand) have been virgins before marrying, or have had a conviction to become abstinent after losing their virginity (what some call being a "born-again virgin," though I reject that term) and actually stuck with it prior to marriage. It's almost like they are unicorns in our culture, because, I'll be the first to admit, it's hard! It takes courage and A LOT of self-discipline and endurance to abstain from something that not only do most people around us do, but that your flesh tells you that you should do, too. And there were times when I didn't even understand why I had the conviction to wait. It felt like a curse. That made for some difficult times.

Thank God for my season of hardship, struggle, and (ultimately) transformation. To be clear, I believe God wants everyone to wait until marriage—there are plenty of Bible verses to support it in the New and Old Testament—but He does not put that *calling* on everyone to wait. That conviction isn't inside all of us, and I discovered that early, which is why at one time it felt like a curse. It wasn't until nearly a year after my relationship ended that I started to uncover God's reasons for me waiting. I say "started" to uncover the reasons for me waiting because all of it hasn't fully been revealed to me yet; it's a masterfully designed process. But I had to go through some things as a consequence of me not waiting, and there were some invaluable lessons learned, so I choose not to regret any of it. It's preparing me for my next season.

Envy

As a person who is called to wait to have sex until marriage, I can say with full transparency that it is not easy watching others get what they want from a relationship perspective when I know for a fact that they didn't have to wait, to abstain from sex, to get it. It takes patience and courage to keep your stance when you don't see any tangible evidence or results from your obedience . . . yet. And yes, it takes patience and courage to trust yourself and your own ability to hear God speaking to you when you have so many other voices clamoring for your attention. And absolutely, it takes patience and courage to keep pressing forward when that little green man called envy is sitting on your shoulder, begging you to look at that thing you want so badly, the one that everyone else around you *seems* to have.

> Don't envy sinners, but always continue to fear the Lord. You will be rewarded for this; your hope will not be disappointed.
>
> —Proverbs 23:17–18 (NLT)

This process of waiting forced me to be still, and also to have the courage to look within, another scary process. As I looked harder, I saw another sin staring me in the face, and it was envy. As I waited, and continue to wait, I uncovered that I tend to envy others around me getting what I desire. Then God led me to these verses in Proverbs 23. He revealed that I should first acknowledge that each and every one of us is a sinner, so none of us is in any place to envy someone else. Additionally, my only concern and focus should be on how I am pleasing God. That's it.

There are two important messages I had to really understand while seeking out God's will for my life during this waiting time, ones that I still have to go back to when I get weak: 1) Other people's relationships are none of my business. What God has for them is for them and what God has for me is for me. One has nothing to do with the other. 2) In Jeremiah 29:11 (NLT), it says, "For I know the plans I have for you, says the Lord. They are plans for good and not for disaster, to give you a future and a hope." This was not just a message for the people of Israel. This was a message for you and me, too.

My assignment is to trust Him and His plans for me and to understand that my convictions are in alignment with those plans. If I choose to follow everyone else, to be disobedient and ignore the convictions He's placed inside me, I'm also choosing to forfeit His plans for me as well. Ouch, that's a scary thought! Perhaps we need to be more careful with that whole free will thing.

Don't copy the behavior and customs of this world, but let God transform you into a new person by changing the way you think. Then you will learn to know God's will for you, which is good and pleasing and perfect.

—Romans 12:2 (NLT)

REFLECTIONS

REFLECTIONS

Free Will

Journal Entry (December 1, 2015)

I read in chapter 3 of Galatians this morning about Paul making a comparison or analogy between Hagar (Abraham's slave wife) and Sarah (his free wife) with people who were enslaved to the law (Jews) and those who were free (followers of Christ). He said Hagar represented a human attempt to fulfill God's promises. I fear that is me. Sarah was getting tired of waiting on God's promise to give her and Abraham children, so she took it upon herself to give her slave to her husband to have a child to secure her and her husband's inheritance. Not too long after, Sarah became pregnant herself.

I wonder how many of God's blessings I've delayed by my own attempt to bring His promise to fruition. I say delay because I know that nothing I could ever do would have the power to derail or change

God's plans. If there's one thing I've learned in my spiritual journey, it's certainly that. I do wonder though what my inability to sit still has cost me. As I continue to read through my journal entries, I realize more and more how impatient I am and how bad I've been over the years at just being still and waiting. It's hard for me to balance the urge and natural instincts to want to make things happen (a noble trait in business) with being still and waiting on God.

But wait, God said faith without works is dead, right? A closed mouth doesn't get fed, right? God might not have said that last statement, but I could go on and on. The bottom line is, I need more discernment during the times when I'm faced with the decision to be proactive or patient. I can't even say reactive, because that's not what God wants me to be. He wants me to listen. He wants me to be obedient. He wants me to let Him lead me instead of the other way around. He wants me to wait on Him.

Perhaps that's where I've failed in the past in relationships. I was trying to lead the man. I didn't necessarily want to, but I felt like I had to because he wasn't doing it. Instead of realizing that the man's reluctance meant I should not just be still and wait for him, but that I should in fact run away, I went full speed ahead at pushing something that wasn't meant to be. Who knows how many Sleeping Adams I have forfeited over the years? [See Sleeping Adam chapter for an explanation of this term.]

It ends here. I'm tired. I shouldn't even say I'm tired of waiting, because I haven't sat still long enough to really wait. I'm tired of attempting in my own human strength to fulfill God's promises. It leads to a dead end every time, and I only end up frustrated, confused, and disappointed as a result of it anyway—the exact opposite of how I want to feel. So I declare TODAY that it ends here. Not that I had it anyway, lol, but God, I relinquish control. I surrender. I apologize for having the gall, pride, and audacity to think that I needed to help You along in the plan for my life. I apologize for not coming to You before putting my "bright ideas" into action. I vow to ALWAYS consult You first before acting, ESPECIALLY as it relates to men.

This is a powerful moment for me because I believe beyond a shadow of a doubt that this shift will cause a breakthrough for me in the coming year, and I receive it! In 2016 I will look back and say December 1, 2015 was a pivotal day for me. Thank you, Father, for this revelation. Amen!

It's safe to say I was feeling quite empowered after that journal entry (insert chuckle and eye roll here). I don't believe I'm the only one who feels some type of accomplishment or pride when I've uncovered a blind spot that's been causing reoccurring issues in my life. As humans, we've all wrestled with free will a time or two. There is certainly a blessing and a curse to it. The blessing is, God created us in His image, so He gave us the power and autonomy to choose and make decisions for ourselves. It is a curse because we are imperfect beings with imperfect and limited ways of thinking, so that power can be dangerous. Why? Because apart from Him, we are clueless.

Have you ever wondered if there is a guidebook for this thing called being an adult? Where is the *How to Successfully Be an Adult for Dummies* manual? Well, there actually is one. It's called the Bible. There's plenty of good stuff in there on how to live, but we're missing it. At least I know I've missed it. When I've needed His instructions the most, I've either gone elsewhere for counsel (not always a bad thing, depending on who you consult) or consulted my own feelings and thought processes at the time, which is always a dangerous thing to do, especially when you're "in your feelings."

> I will teach you wisdom's ways and lead you in straight paths. When you walk, you won't be held back; when you run, you won't stumble. Take hold of my instructions; don't let them go. Guard them, for they are the key to life.
>
> —Proverbs 4:11–13 (NLT)

Where Do I Start?

Some may say, I have a hard time reading the Bible and applying it to my own life. I believe the remedy for that starts with two very simple verses from Proverbs:

> Trust in the Lord with all your heart; do not depend on your own understanding. Seek his will in all you do, and he will show you which path to take.
>
> —Proverbs 3:5–6 (NLT)

If we all truly followed these instructions, we'd save ourselves a lot of heartache. Would we solve all the world's problems if we all did this? Probably not, but it's certainly a start to solving our own. I tried breaking these verses down a little bit more so we could really understand free will and how we should use it.

Trust in the Lord with all your heart

First, we must believe that God is who He says He is. If He is the all-powerful, omniscient, omnipresent creator of the universe we believe He is, shouldn't we trust Him with our lives? We should, but the truth of the matter is, most of us don't.

Why is that? Is it because we can't physically see Him? Or, perhaps, is it because we can't really hear Him because we haven't learned how to discern His voice from our own? Maybe we don't know what trusting Him actually looks like. Perhaps we are just control freaks. Maybe it's all of the above. Whatever the reason or excuse, we've got to give it up, because God has commanded us to trust Him—for our own good, by the way. It wasn't a suggestion.

> Don't let your hearts be troubled. Trust in God, and trust also in me.
>
> —John 14:1 (NLT)

So, what does trusting Him look like? Going back to the story above with Sarah and Hagar, Sarah wanted to have a child. In fact, God promised Sarah and Abraham that not only would they have a child, they would have more descendants than they could count. Trusting God would have looked like Sarah taking a seat and waiting on God to provide her that child He promised her—yes, even in her old age.

I know I'm not the only one who can relate to Sarah taking matters into her own hands when she didn't see God working fast enough. We don't have His omniscient view of the universe, so we can't see why He may have delayed some things we want right now. But if we just trusted Him more and reacted less based off of our own understanding, perhaps we would start to see the divine ways in which God works in our lives BEFORE the mistakes are made and the subsequent heartbreaks occur. The conversation typically goes something like this:

God: Trust Me, I've got this.

Me: But do you really? I think I should do this. Give me a sign, Lord.

God: No, just trust Me.

Me: But God . . .

God: . . . I'll wait . . . [silence]

Me: Okay, I'm just going to do it because I know you want me to have it. Maybe you were just waiting on me to have the courage to do it. Time is running out and I read an article in a magazine that told me that life is too short and I should go after it. YOLO! There's my sign!

God: SMH (shaking my head)

Do not depend on your own understanding

Boy, this is a tough one. God gave us these phenomenal brains with a huge capacity to think and reason and create, and yet we are supposed to put our understanding of things aside when it comes to making decisions for our lives? How does that work? I've certainly had my fair share of struggle with this one. This is where developing a relationship with God comes into play.

Have you ever noticed that when you've known someone a long time and you've spent a lot of time with them, you start to talk and act and ultimately, sometimes, even think like them? (And this is a critical reason why we need to watch who we hang around.) Yep, that's what happens when you develop a relationship with God. You begin to act and think more like Him and less like you.

Will we ever be able to completely act and think like God? Absolutely not, because we're flawed human beings. But when we spend so much time with Him that we start to reason and respond like Him, we'll get that much better at discerning His understanding versus our own, particularly when challenges arise.

> Teach me your ways, O Lord, that I may live according to your truth! Grant me purity of heart, so that I may honor you.
>
> —Psalm 86:11 (NLT)

Seek his will in all you do

If you're anything like me, you do well at seeking Him *sometimes*. It's the "all the time" that is the challenge. I used to mock the really spiritual people who had to pray over EVERY thing they did.

But I'm finding more and more, as I walk in my spiritual journey, that there is something to seeking Him and consulting Him in ALL that I do. And here's the thing: if I can't trust Him and seek Him in the little things I do, how can I trust and seek Him in the big things I do? And conversely, if He can't trust us to pass the small faith tests, are we perhaps delaying the manifestation of larger faith tests?

I know I've struggled with this one because of that issue with patience. When you couple my inherent difficulty with patience along with being an entrepreneur who needs to know how to make decisions quickly, the act of praying and waiting on God to provide an answer feels counterintuitive to my whole process of doing things. I have to admit, I haven't mastered this, but the more I build a relationship with Him and talk to Him constantly, the more He teaches me about how to seek and follow His will in not just some, but in all areas of my life.

Here's another thing I've learned. When you begin to really get tight with God, you'll start to hear the Holy Spirit's voice all the time. It will be a part of you and you'll be able to discern quicker what God's will is for you at any given moment. Now, this requires the highest level of spiritual maturity possible, but it is available to us. I'll delve a little deeper into this point in a later chapter, but for now, meditate on this scripture and pray this prayer to God every day until you memorize it:

Teach me to do your will, for you are my God. May your gracious Spirit lead me forward on a firm footing.

—Psalm 143:10 (NLT)

He will show you which path to take

The order of these verses is important. I didn't notice this until I started studying it, but God doesn't reveal next steps or make a clear pathway until we've made the decision to first trust Him, stop leaning on our own understanding, and seek Him.

If we haven't done our part, how can we expect for Him to do His? If we haven't done all, or even any, of those things in the order in which He has asked, we cannot and should not expect for God to reveal which path He wants us to take. Remember that life collaboration thing? No wonder we are so lost! We're jumping around from one bad decision to the next because we aren't following instructions. We aren't coachable. There's a process to this and we've missed it because we've been so busy reveling in our "free will." Free will was a gift we were given from God to use responsibly and wisely.

The Lord says, "I will guide you along the best pathway for your life. I will advise you and watch over you. Do not be like a senseless horse or mule that needs a bit and bridle to keep it under control."

—Psalm 32:8–9 (NLT)

The Bible says very clearly that God will show us which path to take. I know beyond a shadow of a doubt that every time I've followed God's coaching on this, His plan was revealed very clearly to me. I didn't always like what He was showing me or what that meant I had to do, but I at least had a clear direction, and in hindsight, it was what was best for me.

Some may not understand this next part, but there is a hard reality here. Just because you've followed God's instructions and the next steps on the path were made clear, and it is a part of God's best plan for you, it doesn't mean that what follows is going to be all peaches and cream, or that we'll fully understand it or like it. The next part of the road may be rocky. There might be more challenges you need to go through to get to your desired place.

Look at what happened to Job. He did all he was asked to do; he was obedient, but literally EVERYTHING was taken from him except his life. After all of the hardship he experienced, hardship that would bring the strongest person in the world to their knees, he passed the tests that were thrown at him and eventually he arrived at the other side of his pain. What was waiting for him on the other side was a season of blessings upon blessings that were even greater than the ones he had received prior to his hardship.

In the end, his story was one of the most powerful testimonials in the Bible of obedience and trust in God and has inspired and continues to inspire generations of people for centuries. Job may not have understood it at the time, and perhaps he never knew the full extent of why he went through what he went through, but the point is, he remained obedient and faithful through it all, and ultimately, he was rewarded for it.

The Lord directs our steps, so why try to understand everything along the way?

—Proverbs 20:24 (NLT)

REFLECTIONS

REFLECTIONS

Spiritual Warfare

Journal Entry (December 3, 2015)

I believe I am in the midst of spiritual warfare. I find it hard to get up in the mornings. I literally have to fight discouragement with what sometimes feels like lying to myself. I'm starting to believe that every time it looks like I take two steps forward, I go three steps back—not just in one area, but in several areas of my life. I have thoughts that I shouldn't be having, like, am I really good enough to get the things I desire? These are not my thoughts. And they certainly aren't God's thoughts. So I've come to the conclusion that they belong to the enemy. And it's got to stop.

I uttered a few moments ago that I believe God is letting this happen because He's testing me again to see how I'm going to handle this. I thought to myself, another test? Really, God? I thought I had already prayed this prayer for You to help me fight this enemy. I thought we already kicked him out of my space a few weeks ago. Then I realized, no, this is actually a continuous battle, and I have to lean on God's strength, wisdom, power, and understanding every day if I want to win this war.

Calling on God to fight this battle is an easy thing to do, but it's also an easy thing not to do. I know because I've let it happen. I think that, because the enemy is attacking me again, calling out to God didn't work the first time. No, it works every time, I just haven't done it every time—called out to God, that is. I go off and try to fix it myself. The enemy is very slick and conniving. He knows my weaknesses and where I've failed before. But he's underestimated my faith. I've figured out his strategy and I'm falling for it no more. So I'll just end it here. Help me, Lord! You know what to do. ☺

> So be truly glad. There is wonderful joy ahead, even though you have to endure many trials for a little while. These trials will show that your faith is genuine. It is being tested as fire tests and purifies gold—though your faith is far more precious than mere gold. So when your faith remains strong through many trials, it will bring you much praise and glory and honor on the day when Jesus Christ is revealed to the whole world.
>
> —1 Peter 1:6–7 (NLT)

If you are a Christian and you've lived long enough, you've experienced spiritual warfare at some point in your life. I really didn't know what to call it when I experienced it until one of my small-group sisters pointed it out to me. Once she explained to me what it was, I was blown away. It really put some things into perspective for me as I struggled with what felt like an attack—and it was.

Sometimes the hardship and struggle we go through is brought on by some disobedience or wrong move in the form of a consequence of our actions. Other times it is allowed by God to test us and teach us some really important lessons that we wouldn't otherwise learn without the struggle. In the latter case, sometimes God lets the enemy have his way with us so we can learn how to truly lean on Him for understanding, strength, and wisdom in the midst of trials. In any of those cases, we have to be ready to identify what the attack is, how God wants us to handle it, and the weapons with which He's given us to fight back.

> Put on all of God's armor so that you will be able to stand firm against all strategies of the devil.
>
> —Ephesians 6:11 (NLT)

I must say, when I began this journey, I was ill-equipped for the attack. As I've said before, outside of having to witness my father dying from cancer and some other close people pass away, I've lived a pretty charmed life. Up until that point I had experienced disappointment and a few broken hearts from relationships ending, but I don't believe I had gone through a spiritual attack before. And because I hadn't gone through it before, I took it personally . . . literally. I thought there was something wrong with me. I considered at one point that I might be going through an early mid-life crisis (yes, at thirty-five; again, don't judge me).

As I delved deeper into the Bible and really studied it for myself, and with the help of some amazing spiritual mentors, I began to see clearly what and who it was I was fighting. Once you have that information, I believe half the battle is already won, because then you know how to fight it and what weapons you should use. Ephesians 6:12–18 gives some guidance on the weapons you should use and exactly how to use them against your enemy.

Out of all the valuable insights and lessons learned throughout this process (and there were many), by far the most valuable, rewarding, and useful thing I learned was myself. With each negative thought and bad attitude with which I struggled, I got to know myself a little better. God taught me about some weaknesses I didn't even know I had, and He also reminded me about some strengths I had taken for granted. Had I not gone through this spiritual attack, I would not have gained wisdom or built muscles in those areas where I desperately needed them. And only God knows what else that season prepared me to conquer in the future.

THE ARMOR OF GOD

SPIRITUAL WARFARE WORKSHOP
WITH JENNIFER LUCY TYLER

Ephesians 6:11-20

BELT OF TRUTH
Gird yourself with God's truth. Wrap it firmly around yourself.

BREASTPLATE OF RIGHTEOUSNESS
Maintain integrity and be obedient to God's commands. The Holy Spirit dwells inside of you washing away the old.

SHOES OF READINESS
Always be ready to share the Gospel and keep doing God's work.

SHIELD OF FAITH
Our faith is in God and He is our refuge and strength. We stand on that faith believing that God will conquer and prevail.

HELMET OF SALVATION
The cost has been paid and our salvation is in Jesus. Nothing can separate us from His love.

SWORD OF THE SPIRIT
The word of God is our standard of truth which slays any attempt of deceit and exposes it for what it is.

JENNIFERLUCYTYLER.COM

Credit: Jennifer Lucy Tyler

There must come a time when you and I realize that God really knows what He's doing, so we might as well learn from the hardship, whether we knowingly participated in its existence or not. This was an "aha" moment for me.

So, what did I do to ease the pain when I was going through this difficult season of spiritual warfare? At first, to be honest, I cried . . . a lot. I watched a good amount of TV, specifically movies, to escape having to think about all the issues that were weighing on me. Once I realized the binge sessions distracted my battered mind and soothed my wounded heart for only a few hours at a time, I decided to get myself together and take it to my Father in prayer. He revealed to me a few insights that I still reference whenever I believe I'm going through a spiritual warfare season. Before I get into that, though, I think it's important to understand exactly what spiritual warfare is.

What Is Spiritual Warfare?

The first distinction I had to learn was that while spiritual warfare often takes place during times of tragedy and hardship, the tragedy and hardship itself is not the spiritual warfare. Spiritual warfare occurs when the enemy—also known as Satan, the devil, Beelzebub himself—wages an attack on a spirit; and not just any spirit, a spirit that belongs to the Lord. There is a reason why he is called the enemy; he is the antithesis to everything good, everything the Lord represents. And most times his strategy, which is the most effective strategy out there when it comes to warfare, is to wage an attack during our weakest moments. Think about it; isn't that the best time to wage an advance against an enemy in a natural war?

Just like in any war, when an advance is made, the opponent fights back. The second distinction I learned about spiritual warfare is that, once I discovered how to access the "God in me," I had the power to fight back and win every battle. And it is still a fight, whether we like it or not. But if we stay ready, we don't ever have to get ready. Amen!

Preparation for Promotion

Since that time in late 2015, I've had more seasons of spiritual warfare, and I believe each one of them came just before a season of promotion. When I say promotion, I'm not necessarily talking about the traditional use of the word promotion, as in being elevated into a new role or position, although that has happened as well. I'm talking about promotion in the sense of being elevated to a new place in my life. For example, one of those seasons of spiritual warfare over the last few years has led to me uncovering one of the first levels of my purpose, which has consequently led to me completing this book you are now reading.

I had to recognize the trend. In hindsight, I began to see that every time God was preparing me for a new level, whether it be business/career, relationship, or spiritual (especially spiritual), the enemy staged a major attack—that I believe ultimately prepared me for the magnitude of the promotion. See, the enemy never wants you to get promoted because he knows that strengthens you and makes you harder to fight. But God knows the enemy's schemes, and He also knows what that strengthening process will do for us in allowing us to prepare for our next level. With each new level, however, it requires us to wage an elevated level of defense.

> Dear brothers and sisters, when troubles come your way, consider it an opportunity for great joy. For you know that when your faith is tested, your endurance has a chance to grow.
>
> —James 1:2–3 (NLT)

First, it was imperative that I learned how to access my joy during this season. The enemy hates to see us full of joy because it's harder to distract us. It's easy for him to step in and take control of us when our spirits are heavy, because we're weak. Our defenses are down. When our defenses are down, we'll sometimes do some pretty destructive things to feel better, even if we know it's just for a moment. But Nehemiah 8:10 says the joy of the Lord IS our strength. That means we can actually use joy as a weapon against the enemy!

If that was not reason enough, I knew I could be joyful because the trend told me that my winning season was just around the corner. If I could get to the other side of this spiritual warfare, experience taught me that some type of extraordinary promotion waited for me at the other end.

But the trick is not just getting to the other side of the warfare. After all, this is a preparation season for your promotion, so it does matter *how* you get to the other side. We can't get there kicking and screaming, resistant to the lessons God wants us to learn through the process, if we want to be fully prepared for the promotion. So, the first level of defense I found was joy. Then I had to dig deeper.

Fasting to Focus

One of the activities that has challenged me during my spiritual walk over the years is fasting. I never really understood the point of it. Sure, I read how in the Bible Jesus and His disciples did it, but I didn't really understand a purpose for it in my life until I seriously committed to it during my first identified season of spiritual warfare.

I admit, I still have a lot to learn about fasting, but one of the most critical things I learned about it was how your denial of something you typically include as a daily part of your life helps you to focus on God. Every time I craved or desired that thing I gave up, I went to God, and He sustained me through that season. In many ways I could hear Him clearer. It was as if He didn't have to fight through as much noise as usual to get to me.

I also learned that food is not the only thing from which you can fast. In fact, while abstaining from food altogether or a particular food group or item is the most common practice, there are many other items from which you can abstain, particularly in this day and age, that equally serve the purpose of fasting. We have become so dependent on things like television, social media, shopping, etc., that it has become quite easy to lose our focus on God. Therefore, just giving up one of them for a period of time can make a huge difference in someone's spiritual life.

I'll speak for myself. Remember when I told you how my first reaction when hit with spiritual warfare was to go to the television, movies specifically? Well, guess what I decided to give up for my fast? And it wasn't like I watched a whole lot of TV before. In fact, even back then, occasionally days would go by and I wouldn't even turn it on. But when I considered the fact that it was one of the first things I turned to when I felt the challenges and pressure of an attack, instead of turning to God for comfort and wisdom, I had to evaluate that. I had to wonder why that was my go-to comforter instead of Jesus. And I realized, once I fasted from it, how dependent on it I was to escape the issues that weighed on me . . . if only for a moment.

Once I saw Jesus as my escape route, not only did I get comfort, I got peace. I got counsel. I got love—real, unconditional love. I even got some answers I was seeking, which was priceless, because that led to hope. The television could offer none of that. Once I replaced my focal point, I started to fight my way out of the dark place I had let myself sink into, and I had the strength and armor I needed to fight the real enemy who had hidden himself behind my sorrows.

Covering in Counsel

One of the other critical resources for me during this time was wise counsel. Beyond the good stuff that God was giving me during my quiet time and meditation, I needed strong counselors in my life who had been through what I had been through and could guide me to a better place mentally, emotionally, and spiritually. Sometimes this can be one of the hardest things to do. If you're someone like me who doesn't like to broadcast when things are not going well, this requires you to be vulnerable and ask for help, which can be extremely uncomfortable.

I'm grateful for the multitude of counselors in my life who comforted me with their words of wisdom and assured me that, while it didn't feel like it at the moment, God was doing a good thing in me. They helped me to discern the lessons I couldn't discern on my own and gave me the encouraging words from God I needed to hear out loud. I looked to them as God's messengers, angels so to speak, that helped to decipher and convey God's messages to me and make them clear.

Without guidance, a people will fall, but with many counselors there is deliverance.

—Proverbs 11:14 (CSB)

I would have felt a bit lost without them, because in that moment, I didn't have a lot of confidence in my feelings or in my own discernment. I'm one of those people who is more critical of themselves than anyone else ever could be, and I beat myself up a lot. It was helpful to have people in my corner who didn't jump on the bandwagon with my inner critic, but who could also be straight with me about the hard lessons I needed to learn. You need people like that in your life, but a word of caution: you must qualify those people in your life before you give them that type of power. That role of counselor is not meant to be played by everyone.

Turn to God First

Even when you do have a multitude of wise counselors in your life whose wisdom you trust and whom you believe have your best interest at heart, I want to leave you with this last word of caution when encountering spiritual warfare: Go to God first.

When presented with troubling circumstances or a situation where you have to make a decision and you are not sure which way to turn, it's best not to talk to anyone about it until you talk to God first. There are a few reasons for this: 1) That person cannot possibly have the full picture; therefore, they cannot offer words of wisdom based on the bigger picture. Only God can provide insight from the perspective of the bigger picture, based on what was behind and what is to come. 2) They are offering advice, even with the best intentions possible, from a filtered lens, no matter how enlightened or nonjudgmental they are. 3) If you get advice or recommendations that are not in your best interest, especially if it is coming from multiple sources, you will only be confused.

Sometimes God speaks through other people for you to hear, but if that voice is not God's voice and you aren't developed enough spiritually to discern God's voice from another, it may only confuse you, or worse, send you in the wrong direction, off-course of God's plans for you.

When met with spiritual warfare, first identify what it is, then go to God's word—start with Ephesians 6:12–18—and put yourself in a place where you can hear from God about your next steps. If you don't hear anything at first, don't be alarmed and don't give up. Just keep listening and He'll find a way for you to hear, if you are willing. Remember, we're all promised troubles; it's the "but God" that gives us hope for what's on the other side of our troubles.

Good people suffer many troubles, but the Lord saves them from them all.

—Psalm 34:19 (GNT)

REFLECTIONS

REFLECTIONS

purpose

Journal Entry (December 7, 2015)

Your hope should not be based on your understanding of God's purpose for you. Rather, your faith should be firmly grounded in God, who is bringing it about in you. Even if that purpose seems distant, you still trust Him to bring you to the destination successfully.

(<u>Moments of Peace</u>, evening devotion for December 5)

I've been thinking more and more about my purpose lately. And as we approach the new year, I've been more contemplative about what that new year will bring as far as business and new opportunities are concerned. I have to admit, I've been a little afraid because God hasn't revealed a whole lot yet. Then I read this devotional from December 5. It puts some things in perspective, though ultimately, it's telling me the same things I've heard in this season of my life. Stay close to God, listen, be obedient, and continue to have faith and trust in Him. It sounds so easy, right? But sometimes it's the hardest thing to do. Perhaps that's why I keep getting the same messages over and over again. God wants to drill it in. I need it when those doubts from the enemy creep in. And the Lord knows I've had my fair share of them, especially this year.

One thing I do need to do though is spend some dedicated time with God to talk about what He wants me to do in the new year. I've never done that before. I've always told Him what I wanted to have happen and then asked Him to bless it and bring it to fruition. It sounds silly now that I think about it, but it's that mindset that's gotten me to where I am in this moment, so I'm deciding to do something different. Perhaps now I'll get different results.

> For we are God's masterpiece. He has created us anew in Christ Jesus, so we can do the good things he planned for us long ago.
>
> —Ephesians 2:10 (NLT)

Discovery of Purpose

I think it's a travesty that some people wander aimlessly throughout their entire lives, never bothering to figure out why they were put on this Earth, what assignments they have. And if anyone thinks they don't have a unique purpose, they don't know God very well. In the Ephesians 2:10 scripture above, it says each of us are God's masterpiece. In some translations, it reads His workmanship. That means we are all intentionally here, designed for a specific purpose. There is nothing and no one on this Earth that did not originate from a thought in God's mind, so you belong here for a reason.

> You made all the delicate, inner parts of my body and knit me together in my mother's womb. Thank you for making me so wonderfully complex! Your workmanship is marvelous—how well I know it. You watched me as I was being formed in utter seclusion, as I was woven together in the dark of the womb. You saw me before I was born. Every day of my life was recorded in your book. Every moment was laid out before a single day had passed.
>
> —Psalm 139:13–16 (NLT)

Some people discover and become clear on their purpose early in life and bless others by walking in that purpose for the majority of their time here on Earth, however long that may be. For others, for most I would argue, it takes some time. If that person is you, don't be discouraged. If we truly believe that God is as amazing as He says He is, and if He was able to give Abraham and Sarah the manifestation of their purpose (a child for them) in their old age, He can certainly do the same for you.

At the time of my life when I wrote this journal entry, in my mid-thirties, I was well aware I had an assignment, I just hadn't quite been able to pinpoint it yet. And the older I got, the more disappointed I felt from the lack of revelation. If you're anything like me, this will be a familiar situation. I think the majority of us, especially Christians, live in that space. And it's not necessarily that God is hiding the answer to that question; sometimes it just requires a certain level of trust, faith, and closeness to God that we haven't mastered yet in order to discover it.

As I began to study myself and my behavior throughout this journal writing process, I found that disobedience is one of the hindrances to discovering our purpose. With each step we take in the opposite direction of what God tells us to do, we take a step away from God and, ultimately, from the road that leads us toward discovering and walking in our assignment. No wonder many of us are still wandering aimlessly without a sense of purpose! God provides the pathway; we're just inadvertently deciding to go in a different direction when we choose to disobey.

Think of this process in terms of that game of "Hot & Cold" many of us played as children. Remember how, as you got closer to or further away from a hidden object, your friends would give you a temperature to describe how close you were to finding it? As God gives us direction and we obey, God is saying "you're getting warmer." Conversely, when we disobey, God says "you're freezing." If we first seek and then obey instruction from God, I believe that's going to get us closer to winning the prize of finding our purpose.

It wasn't until two years after writing this journal entry that I finally heard God's voice, loud and clear, give me some direction on my assignment. And it was during a time of deep reflection and, most importantly, strict obedience. At the time, I wanted a situation, a relationship, to go in a different direction than it was going, but instead of trying to fix the situation or manipulating it to go the way I wanted it to go, like I had done in the past, I just simply got quiet and still and started listening. (I'll share more on that in just a minute.) I was fully submitted. And just like that, God gave me some big news. That was the beginning of my ministry.

Ironically enough, I had already started writing this book, but I had taken a nearly year-long hiatus. Once the vision of my assignment became clear, I got focused and I started writing again. All of a sudden, I had purpose. I wasn't just writing to share my story and perhaps to inspire people; I was writing to help save people's lives and their relationships with Christ. Communicating with people about their relationship with Christ through my writing and speaking became my ministry. I found my why, and suddenly I felt like I had put two big puzzle pieces together.

> There is a single unique space in the universe that no shape other than yours can fit into. When you find your

purpose and walk in it, you fit perfectly into that space and the whole world will take shape around you.

—Touré Roberts

That decision I made when writing that journal entry on December 7, 2015, to take time to sit down with God and let Him reveal to me what He wanted me to do in the new year, was a defining moment for me. Even though it didn't manifest right away, and it took me some time to really understand what that looked like from a practical standpoint, it was the beginning of a transformational moment for me that wouldn't start to really take shape in the physical sense for another two years. I had to wait for it, which I just so happened to have a lot of practice in.

A lot of people struggle with purpose (I believe now, having been someone who struggled with it for as long as I did) because we haven't fully given ourselves over to the transformation it requires of us to fully accept it. Particularly if you are an adult going through the discovery process of your purpose, like most are, it will require you to think a bit differently and do things a bit differently than you've done before. And I know I don't have to tell you change is hard.

Debunking the Myth

> The way we keep our greatness out of the graveyard of potential is by submitting ourselves to the process of transformation that God has orchestrated for our lives.
>
> —Touré Roberts

Remember when I said this purpose discovery process came at a time of deep reflection and obedience? It was transformational because I was fully submitted. I started to read the book *Purpose Awakening* by Touré Roberts (which I reference in the two quotes above), and I started to not just do the work, but to also submit to the transformation process God was beginning in me.

In full transparency, this transformation process was happening during a time when I was experiencing hardship, struggle, and disappointment in a relationship that I just knew in the beginning was God-sent and ordained. (And perhaps this relationship was both, but not for the reasons I originally thought.) I thought I had learned the lessons and now, in 2017, I was going to get the reward for my obedience. Yet, as seemingly suddenly and unexpectedly as the relationship began, it started to unravel in the same fashion. Unbelievably, I had found myself emotionally in the same place I found myself on the eve of 2015—confused, heartbroken, disappointed—even after being obedient and doing things "the right way" this time, or so I thought. But the good news was that I was in a perfect place to listen and receive.

The difference between 2015 and 2017 was in how I chose to handle that disappointment, confusion, and heartbreak, and that made all the difference. Instead of retreating and wallowing in self-pity, I got close to God immediately. Rather than drawing on my own understanding, I rested in His. Instead of doing what I could do to manipulate the situation and "fix" things in order to make me and my boyfriend feel better, I drew from God's joy and peace and solely focused on fully submitting to Him. All of a sudden, my recovering, people-pleasing spirit no longer had power over me. I stopped trying to do everything I could to please the person with whom I was in a relationship and I just let go. I let God work on me. Ultimately, I lost my boyfriend, the man I mistakenly thought would be my husband, but I found my purpose. So, I guess you could say I was winning!

I share that story because a lot of people mistakenly believe that the process of discovering and walking in your purpose is supposed to be easy, or at least comfortable. On the contrary, for many it is anything but easy or comfortable, and oftentimes it comes during seasons of complete despair and defeat. This process is challenging and involves some stretching.

Don't get me wrong, I'm not saying that someone has to go through a breakup or some other traumatic experience in order to get to their purpose. What I am saying is that the road to getting there is not always straight, smooth, or without some speedbumps and detours. It will require you to transform, in whatever way that looks like for you, to get to the other side.

Deciding to Walk

The decision you make to walk in purpose is a whole other step beyond the discovery. This requires a whole new level of action steps and faith. It's hard because God doesn't always reveal the whole path at first, just what's necessary for the first few steps. Then, when we've accomplished that, He reveals a little bit more.

Remember, in my chapter on "The Wait," the fog I talked about? I believe now, as I've gone through this process and as I'm still in the midst of it, that if God showed us a clear picture of everything we need to go through to get to our purpose, we probably wouldn't take those first few steps. Sometimes we need to be eased into things, particularly as it relates to purpose. The good news is, when we are attuned to His voice and consciously choose to walk in obedience, no matter what, we can have 100 percent confidence that He will show us the way.

> Whether you turn to the right or to the left, your ears will hear a voice behind you, saying, "This is the way; walk in it."
>
> —Isaiah 30:21 (NIV)

Walking in purpose is a wonderful thing, and I believe it brings true, abundant life in every sense of the word. But it also requires an incredible amount of faith, strength, and endurance, and we have none of those things apart from Him.

The faith, the strength, the endurance we need to pursue and fulfill purpose all come from Him, so that's why we have to get as close to Him as we can to discover it.

REFLECTIONS

REFLECTIONS

Gratefulness

Journal Entry (December 17, 2015)

This is the perfect day to depend on Him with childlike trust.

> Jesus said, "Come to me, all of you who are weary and carry heavy burdens, and I will give you rest. Take my yoke upon you. Let me teach you, because I am humble and gentle at heart, and you will find rest for your souls. For my yoke is easy to bear, and the burden I give you is light."
>
> —Matthew 11:28–30 (NLT)

Father, I thank You for Your endless grace and mercy. I know I am in deep need of it every second of every minute of every day. I thank You for Your provisions and many blessings. I am never in need of anything thanks to Your constant providing of my needs. Even when I can't see around the corner how I'm going to make it through the next day or week or month, You can, and I am extremely grateful for that.

I thank You for not giving up on me. I thank You for continuing to work on me. Sometimes it takes me multiple failures to get it, but I thank You for those multiple opportunities to get it right. I may not like it while I'm in the thick of it, but I'm always pleased with the end result. I'm grateful for this time to get to know myself. I hadn't really taken this much time in prayer and worship time with You before. As a result, I'm discovering more about me and Your light in me. I have so much to contribute to this Earth, and I know now I haven't been living up to my full potential. I pray that You help me with that this year. Help me to discover and peel back the layers of my purpose. Help me to honor You by delving deeper into my purpose. Thank you, Father, Amen.

> How kind the Lord is! How good he is! So merciful, this God of ours! The Lord protects those of childlike faith; I was facing death, and he saved me. Let my soul be at rest again, for the Lord has been good to me.
>
> —Psalm 116:5–7 (NLT)

During that season of hardship, it was important for me to stay grateful for all that God had done. When we are going through hard times, it's easy to continue to pile more heartache on by thinking about what's not going right, what things you don't have, or what God didn't do to make things right. But when you start to think about all of the amazing things that did happen, how God perhaps saved you from something bad that could've happened if you had actually gotten what you prayed for, or just the fact that you're alive and well in spite of your brokenness, your perspective starts to shift.

When I looked back at this journal entry, and I looked at how I began with the statement about childlike trust, I was confused. Why would I talk about childlike trust and then go on to talk about how grateful I am? That morning, one of the devotionals I read, Jesus Calling, spoke about how to deal with feeling empty inside and harboring feelings of inadequacy and sluggishness, which was just what I was feeling at that moment. The devotional encouraged me to make that statement about childlike trust and then continue on with my day embracing that dependence on God, which would in turn bring joy and peace, and ultimately gratitude, by the end of the day. I must have immediately handed my burdens over to God, hence the verse from Matthew 11, and began to feel gratitude almost immediately.

When I think back on how I was feeling in this moment, I envision a child trying to be a big boy or a big girl by carrying a piece of luggage that was really meant to be carried by an adult, but they're struggling with it nonetheless, because they want to do it themselves. Once they've had enough of carrying it on their own, they hand it over to their parent, who picks it up with ease, and immediately a sense of relief overcomes them.

I believe I had that same type of experience. I was struggling to carry some pretty large loads on my own, but once the heavy weight was lifted, I started to realize how much I needed my Father to help me. Once I had that revelation, I could feel nothing but gratitude because I recalled all the other times He had relieved me from my struggle when I just let go.

The Thanksliving Jar

> Be thankful in all circumstances, for this is God's will for you who belong to Christ Jesus.
>
> —1 Thessalonians 5:18 (NLT)

On January 1, 2017, I began a ritual that I've continued to this day that took my daily gratitude to a new level. Upon the suggestion of an *Our Daily Bread* devotional at the end of 2016, I began my Thanksliving Jar project. At the end of each day, I write down the one or two things I am most grateful for that day on a small sheet of paper and I drop it into a glass jar. At the end of the year, I pour out all 365 notes of gratitude and read them.

It sounds simple enough, but I struggled with this activity at first; and to be honest, I still do at times. First, like any new habit, it takes a while before you find your rhythm. Some people say it takes twenty-one days, others say sixty-six, and some even say it requires nearly a year for a person to create a habit. However long it takes—perhaps it's different for everyone—I know it requires time and patience with yourself to become disciplined enough to do something EVERY day consistently. And even when you do, any little change in routine—travel, waking up later than expected, emergencies—can throw that habit off.

Even with only doing this gratitude exercise at first maybe two or three times a week, I started to notice an immediate, though slight, shift in perspective. Moment by moment, week by week, I started to regain some of my peace back that had been chipped away at over the years from the struggles and challenges of just being an adult.

When I think of the saying "sleeping like a baby," I'm reminded of what life must have been like as a child. I think about how much inherent trust I had to have had in my parents to feed me, clothe me, and put a roof over my head. I never had to worry about those things because I knew they were covered. In fact, there was no thought that those things would not be taken care of because I inherently trusted them to do so. Now, having been an adult for some time, I can distinctly remember what it was like to live a life of constant peace as a child. I believe that's the kind of peace God wants us to have as an adult. He wants us to trust so completely in

Him and His ability to cover us that it mimics the type of peace we had as children.

Before I became intentional about my daily gratitude with the Thanksliving jar, I honestly didn't get the connection between gratefulness and peace. But now that it's become a habit, I can tell you with full confidence: there is absolutely a connection. The more grateful you are intentionally, the more evident God's provisions and protection become in your eyes, which eventually brings about trust. When you can fully trust in God's faithfulness, the more at peace you are.

The other challenge I had with this exercise was that when bad things happened, I really had a strong urge to reject doing the exercise. When you're "in your feelings," as we like to say these days, we tend to want to stay in our feelings and wallow in self-pity for a while; at least I do. But when I force myself to be grateful for something in spite of the bad thing or things that happened, it makes me feel uncomfortable because it's the opposite of how I feel.

For example, one day about two months or so into my new Thanksliving Jar habit, I got into a bad car accident. I rear-ended someone on the highway, for which I was at fault, and my car was dinged up so badly it had to be towed to my home. To make matters worse, the insurance company's initial assessment was that the car was likely totaled. I felt so deflated and defeated. The last thing I wanted to do those first couple of hours and days following the accident was write down how grateful I was for anything. In hindsight, obviously I had a lot for which to be grateful—most glaringly the fact that neither I nor the other passengers were injured, and most importantly that we were still alive. Of course, once I really got over myself and my feelings, the gratitude immediately shifted my focus and I found my peace even in the midst of the storm.

I'm not going to paint a pretty picture that portrays gratefulness as the cure-all to life's problems, or say that I haven't since gotten upset or disappointed with life's challenges. What I will say is, being intentionally grateful has allowed me to shift my focus and perspective in those tough moments, and it's brought me more peace than I've ever had as an adult.

Let the peace of Christ rule in your hearts, since as members of one body you were called to peace. And be thankful.

—Colossians 3:15 (NIV)

Being Intentional

You would think, as fortunate as we are, that it would not take work to live a life of gratitude. But somehow along the journey of life, we, especially those of us who identify ourselves as Christians or Christ followers, became entitled. We started believing that because we have faith, because we do the right things (or try to do the right things) most of the time, somehow that means we aren't supposed to go through hardship and challenges. Therefore, when trouble shows up or we lose something or someone dear to us, we get mad, confused, frustrated, and a whole host of other feelings that lead to a lack of gratitude for the things and people we do have. And sometimes it doesn't even have to be a major thing that sends us into an ungratefulness tailspin.

I remember one day, during one of my monthly service visits with friends to a transitional home for women, I was feeling a little down about something. I don't even remember what I was feeling down about—that's how minor it was—and something unexpected snapped me out of it. One of the women who lived there paused as we were serving her, and she said something that stopped me in my tracks, that I will never forget. She said, "Ladies, always remember: Let joy be your go-to emotion." It was so simple, yet so profound. I don't know what brought her to that transitional home, but I know many of the women living there have experienced everything from abusive relationships to drug addictions, health challenges, and worse. We volunteer to serve there in large part to help encourage them and lift their spirits, but that day she gave that gift to us.

She had it right. Experiencing joy, being thankful, and expressing gratitude is all a choice. It is intentional. If we are not careful, we may forget that we still have a lot for which to be grateful. Especially if we have a natural tendency to get in the dumps when things are not going as well as we'd like or hope, we've got to be intentional about our gratitude. It's really the best remedy for a bad mood. It's kind of tough to harbor negative feelings and wallow in self-pity when you are being intentional about expressing gratitude and joy. When you consider that despite all your circumstances you are still alive, and God has given you another day on this Earth, that alone is enough to rejoice in.

This is the day that the Lord has made; let us rejoice and be glad in it.

—Psalm 118:24 (ESV)

REFLECTIONS

REFLECTIONS

My Life Is a Praise Song

Journal Entry (December 20, 2015)

In my devotional this morning it said, "Let your life become a praise song to me..." What would that look like, for me to do that? I don't think I'm far off from that but I do know there are some adjustments I need to make. I need to constantly ask myself the question, "What would be pleasing to God?" "How can I praise/please God by doing this?" That's the next level of praise and worship, and of my (spiritual) walk for that matter. It's time for me to go to the next level. I can't stay here. Perhaps that's my theme for 2016: Next Level. Next level in my spiritual walk, next level in my relationship status, next level in my business. Wow, that just became clear to me, just like that. I prayed for that to be revealed and I am certain I just heard

God speak to me. Thank you, Lord. ☺ *That's how my life becomes a praise song!*

Several years back I started to assign a theme to my year in lieu of making empty, non-inspiring resolutions that I'd quit on midway through the year, and the interesting thing I've found is that the themes have manifested, just not in the way and timing in which I perceived them. They've seemingly lagged behind a year or two. In fact, in this year of 2018, I'm only just now really starting to see the manifestation of this next level theme where my life is becoming a praise song. Sure, as I stated earlier in the "Spiritual Warfare" chapter, I've certainly seen levels of promotion in my life over the past three years that have occurred immediately after spiritual warfare. But it's nothing compared to the "next level" growth that is taking place in my life right now. But that is just how God works—above all we could ever think of or imagine.

> Now to him who is able to do immeasurably more than all we ask or imagine, according to his power that is at work within us . . .
>
> —Ephesians 3:20 (NIV)

When I wrote this journal entry I was pouring out what I was receiving from God, but in hindsight, I really did not understand the magnitude of what any of it meant. I had to go through some things and learn some lessons first. I'm glad I wrote it down, though, because it helped me put some puzzle pieces together.

Now, when I think about what it really means to praise God with my life, it takes on a whole new meaning. God designed me, designed everyone, to do something unique, something that no other person on this Earth was designed to do. When we figure out what that thing or those things are, it's like a whole new world opens up for us.

I know, here I go, talking about purpose again. Don't check out, I promise I'm going somewhere with this. Yes, purpose is a critical piece of what I'm getting to, but what I'm really talking about is the concept of living an abundant life. You know that key verse in John 10:10, where Jesus tells us what the enemy came to do and then He proclaims conversely that He has come so that we might have life abundantly? Yep, that one. Have you ever wondered what that means—to live an abundant life?

I honestly never really took time to break down the concept of what an abundant life meant and looked like until I got a life-changing call from the women's ministry at my church one day in late 2017. The request was for me to serve as a breakout session speaker on the topic of "The Abundant Life." The woman on the other end of the line said, "I'm not even sure if this is something you do, but you came to my mind to speak on this topic." Ironically, that call came only a few weeks after I had the revelation about my purpose. I replied to myself, "Well, it is now."

As a side note, when I had that breakthrough moment in my purpose discovery, God revealed that, as a public relations professional of more than thirteen years, I was about to take on my biggest client EVER . . . HIM. God Himself spoke in words that I could hear. He was setting me on a path in this next phase of life, prompting me to take my unique spiritual gifts and the skillsets I had built over the last several years as an entrepreneur and a publicist—speaking, writing, making connections—and use them now for His glory. He was beginning to elevate me from what I affectionately referred to as "the Golden Life"—my version of living my best life—to "the Abundant Life"—God's version of living my best life.

As I began to prepare my message about the abundant life—this thing that everyone wants, but which always seemed to be so elusive—I realized that the concept wasn't ambiguous at all. I went to Facebook Live to conduct a survey of what my friends thought the abundant life was, and I heard everything from prosperity and wealth to happiness, contentment, and having more than enough of what you need. And to be honest, there was a time in the not-too-distant past when I would have agreed with all of what they were sharing, and the fact that an abundant life means something different to each person.

> I have come that they may have life, and that they may have it more abundantly.
>
> —John 10:10b (NKJV)

And then I went to the Bible. I asked God to show me what He wanted me to share about this Abundant Life concept, since the concept of having life abundantly first appeared in His book anyway. Since we as human beings were created for His glory (Isaiah 43:7), what would abundant life mean to Him with that truth as a reference point? What does an abundant life look like through God's eyes, considering we were created for His glory? Perhaps a praise song?

I concluded that, if we discover and use our unique spiritual gifts that God gave us to serve one another; discover and walk in our unique assignments He planned for us; and learn how to live and walk in the present—not the past or the future, but the right now that He gave us—we can begin to step into and experience that abundant life He promised us. And here's another important point I discovered: living an abundant life has less to do with what we actually attain and more to do with what we can give and how we can be of service to others with what God gave us.

The truth of the matter is, while the byproducts of an abundant life may be varied (wealth and prosperity, peace, happiness, etc.), the formula for achieving it is pretty clear and attainable. While the Bible had many authors who came from different backgrounds and time periods, it was inspired by the word of God and remained consistent on a number of topics—one of them being why we're here and how we are to use our time here.

Over the last several months, since reading the book *Purpose Awakening* that I mentioned above in the "Purpose" chapter, receiving that phone call from the women's ministry at my church, and getting clear on what an abundant life really is, I can say with confidence that I am absolutely living it, and I want others to as well. I want others to experience being able to live their lives as a praise song to the Lord.

Spiritual Gifts

> God has given each of you a gift from his great variety of spiritual gifts. Use them well to serve one another.
>
> —1 Peter 4:10 (NLT)

In breaking down this concept of living an abundant life for the women I ministered to at the conference, I offered the discovery and use of spiritual gifts as one piece of a three-part puzzle. ("Discover & Walk in Purpose" and "Discover & Delight in Your Present" were the other two.) It just made sense to me that, if we were created in God's image and He sent his Son to serve us and give the ultimate sacrifice of His life, we should be well-equipped to glorify Him by serving one another as well.

Did you also notice that Peter said "each" of us, not "some" of us? I've actually talked to believers who don't think they have any spiritual gifts. We may not be aware of them, but God gave each and every one of us spiritual gifts, and they are there for a purpose. I believe some of us are literally sitting on a gold mine of untapped spiritual gifts that are just waiting to be unleashed. And once they are, I believe that is where the abundant life begins.

There are at least four main passages in the Bible that speak to specific spiritual gifts (1 Corinthians 12:8–11, Romans 12:6–8, 1 Peter 4:10–11, and Ephesians 4:11–12). I believe there are other miscellaneous spiritual gifts like hospitality, missionary work, and celibacy that are talked about in other places in scripture, but the majority of spiritual gifts fall into one of those four passages.

Once I really went back and examined and meditated on the results of a spiritual gifts test I took a few years ago, my purpose and accompanying assignments became easier to identify. My top five spiritual gifts of administration, faith, mercy, exhortation, and giving made sense and were perfectly in alignment with what God was revealing to me about my purpose. But let me be clear: I definitely have not arrived. I still have a lot of discovery and growth ahead, but my path became clearer when I identified those previous missing pieces.

If you haven't yet identified what your spiritual gifts are, or if perhaps you have forgotten like I did, I recommend spiritualgiftstest.com as a first step or a reminder. I also recommend doing an exercise I gave to the women in my breakout session at the conference. I had them sit next to someone they knew well or did life with and asked each of them to write down the spiritual gifts of the other. Oftentimes I find others can see certain things about our spiritual gifts to which we may be blind. Additionally, I definitely recommend spending time in prayer and meditation to ask God to reveal to you what your spiritual gifts are and, more importantly, how to use them in glorifying Him and serving others.

Be Present

> Give your entire attention to what God is doing right now, and don't get worked up about what may or may not happen tomorrow. God will help you deal with whatever hard things come up when the time comes.
>
> —Matthew 6:34 (MSG)

As I was meditating on what the concept of abundant life meant, God revealed to me through this scripture in Matthew 6:34 that I had to do a much better job at focusing on the here and now if I wanted to live this abundant life I was called to speak on. I'm going to go ahead and jump out there and say it's not a challenge that is unique to me. I'm going to assume most of us spend way more time than we should wallowing in the past and supposing, worrying about, or over-planning our future.

> You can make many plans, but the Lord's purpose will prevail.

—Proverbs 19:21 (NLT)

There are some of us who live our lives in waiting—waiting for our husbands to find us, waiting to have children, waiting to discover our purpose, waiting for our dream job, waiting for the right time to start that business or write that book, etc. In the meantime, we find ourselves standing still, waiting for our lives to unfold instead of actually living them. And if you aren't waiting, perhaps you're spending a lot of your time planning, which may leave you disappointed a lot, because if you've lived long enough, you'll find life rarely goes exactly how you plan it. If you're in neither category, consider that you may be the one worrying about your future, scared to take that next step because you aren't sure how it's going to turn out—paralyzed by fear.

Then there are others who spend a lot of time in the past, and there can be two sets of people in this category. They either have fond memories that keep them stuck on "the good old days," prohibiting them from doing anything else great because they think their best years are behind them, or they have bad memories that keep them complaining about how unfair life has been, and are thus paralyzed by pain. In either scenario you limit yourself from actually living a full life in the present.

Being someone who typically has found herself teetering between the two ends of the spectrum depending on the season I'm in, I started adopting some practices that have helped me stay in the present, thus allowing me to live a more abundant life. Some of them we've covered in previous chapters, but they're worth mentioning again.

1. Have Daily Gratitude: The more you focus on being grateful for something, or several things, each day, the less you worry about the future or wallow in the past. Remember, there is always something for which we can be grateful, even if it's just the fact that God woke us up and allowed us to see another day.

2. Limit Distractions: We have more distractions these days than at any other time in history. Between social media, cell phones, and technology in general, some of us have been completely conditioned to spend the majority of our lives on our devices. In fact, I read a stat that says the average person cannot go ten minutes without checking their phone, which means we check our phones about eighty times a day. Wow! What if, instead of being glued to our technology, the next time you are waiting for someone, standing in an elevator with people, waiting in line at the grocery store, on public transportation, or in an Uber, you were just present to your surroundings and talked to the people who are in your space? Imagine how much more in tune you would be with your surroundings, and thus how much more focused in the here and now.

3. Purge: I've found that minimalism definitely forces you to live in the present. When we remove items associated with past memories or lives, it frees us up to stop living in the past and start living in the present. What if we gave up the clutter, the old photos and mementos, from past relationships? What if we purged some of our grudges and forgave people in our lives who've hurt us? I believe all of the above could make room and provide space for some new memories, people, or things God is trying to bring into our lives.

4. Breathe: Focusing on your breathing has a lot of benefits, including relaxation and stress relief, but it also helps you to be present. Your breath is always present, happening in the right now, so when you focus on it you have no choice but to be in the present moment—right where God wants you to operate.

5. Practice Joy: As I mentioned before, joy is a choice. Just as we can find a number of things to be thankful for each day, we can always find reasons to choose joy. One way I've been able to access my joy is by staying on top of my self-care. When I do the things that make me feel good, like getting a pedicure, taking a hot bubble bath, or getting my hair done, that brings me joy. When you feel better, you do better, and when you do better, you feel better.

> And it is a good thing to receive wealth from God and the good health to enjoy it. To enjoy your work and accept your lot in life—this is indeed a gift from God. God keeps such people so busy enjoying life that they take no time to brood over the past.
>
> —Ecclesiastes 5:19–20 (NLT)

Once I started making a habit out of these activities, I found myself operating at a higher level. It wasn't that I stopped having challenges or that I started to receive everything I wanted. Instead, I just started to shed the stress and anxiety that kept me from living my best life. Do I sometimes get side-tracked every now and again? Absolutely! I haven't perfected this thing, but my praise song has become sweeter.

REFLECTIONS

REFLECTIONS

God's Will Be Done

Journal Entry (December 23, 2015)

> God's will is not a mystery. He has a wonderful path that He wants you to follow, but you must be willing to do two things. First, ask Him to reveal His plan to you. Second, be committed to obeying Him even if it means making a difficult decision.
>
> Thank you, God for revealing your will to me when I fully place my trust in you. You are faithful and true, and worthy of praise. Amen.
>
> (<u>Moments of Peace</u>, morning devotion for December 23)

That was from my devotional this morning. I forgot that I could ask for God to reveal His will for me. Sometimes I feel like I'm in the dark and I'm just waiting for my life to unfold. It's difficult to prepare for something if you don't know what's coming, so I think I've been resigned in some ways, because I figure if I can't control what's going to happen from one moment to the next, what's the use of preparing and planning? It only leaves me disappointed when things don't go the way I'm expecting them to. But that's where the revelation is. I haven't asked God to reveal His will. I'm not in sync with Him. I'm sort of spinning my wheels, so to speak, and I've had the power to be in sync with Him this whole time as it relates to His will for my life. I know sometimes He's not going to reveal it in my timing, but it is encouraging to know He will reveal it, if I ask. You ask and you shall receive.

Your Wish Is My Command

> If you remain in me and my words remain in you, ask whatever you wish, and it will be done for you.
>
> —John 15:7 (NIV)

This is a powerful scripture, but if taken out of context it can be easily misused and misinterpreted. Once this scripture was truly broken down for me and I began to study and meditate on it for myself, a lot of insight opened for me.

If you only emphasize and pay attention to the last part of the scripture, you will find yourself believing that God is some sort of genie in a bottle and that He's obligated to give us whatever we request. The first part of that verse, however, is quite a significant qualifier: "If you remain in me and my words remain in you . . ."

What this qualifier means to me is that we've got to get to know God *first* before we make our requests. I mean *really* get to know Him. We've got to seek, study, and meditate on His word. We've got to talk to Him and build a relationship with Him. Psalm 37:4 (NIV) says, "Take delight in the Lord, and He will give you the desires of your heart." Delight in the Lord. That means truly enjoy Him by spending quality time with Him. It means opening up our hearts to Him. It means becoming a student of and consuming His word.

I remember a sermon my pastor, Keith Battle, gave on the keys to discerning God's will for one's life, and one of the first points he made was turning to His word. Because the will of God and His word are always going to be in harmony, we can trust that we will get direction on His will by going to His word. They will never contradict each other.

Additionally, in order for us to be in sync and in tune with Him, we must stay connected to Him. Have we truly stopped to consider what that really means, to be connected to Him?

> I am the vine; you are the branches. If you remain in me and I in you, you will bear much fruit; apart from me you can do nothing.
>
> —John 15:5 (NIV)

These passages give us a peek inside the conversation Jesus is having with His disciples where He uses an analogy of a grapevine to explain to them how they should live in Him. What He's saying here is that you've got to be so close to Him, such that you've engrained the words He speaks into your very being, that He and you become connected, become one. You connect at the heart level. Therefore, when you are in one accord with Him, what you ask for will be in alignment with His will.

The tough part here is that many of us have not taken the time to really develop this type of deep relationship with God. That fact is evident in the world, it is evident in our society and culture, and it is evident, sadly, in our churches. The average Christian really only talks to God either when they are praying over their food, maybe when saying quick prayers prior to going to bed or waking up, and/or when they're dealing with a severe hardship or loss. The truth is, if we really want to have the type of relationship with Him that He was referring to in this passage, we've got to go deeper.

This was an epiphany for me during that challenging season. As I was struggling to understand and discover God's will, and feeling helpless while doing it, I discovered part of the reason God had me going through such hardship was because He knew it would draw me closer to Him. I started spending more time with Him. I began to really study His word for myself. I began to consistently have really deep, raw conversations with Him. I meditated. I listened. I wasn't just relying on Sunday sermons and other religious leaders' interpretation of scripture to feed my soul. It was in this place where I began to develop a deeper, more substantive relationship with Him, and also began to uncover how surface level my relationship had been with Him previously. No wonder I felt so lost.

> Ask and it will be given to you; seek and you will find; knock and the door will be opened to you.
>
> —Matthew 7:7 (NIV)

This concept of asking and receiving shows up multiple times in the Bible, but it is a tricky one. Not only is there a qualifier for us to be connected to Him, we also must be obedient and patient. There go those curse words again.

As I began my journey of truly walking with Christ during this time and fine-tuning my ability to discern my own voice from His, I got better at making spiritually mature requests. But after revisiting this devotional and studying some of these other scriptures, I realized that just because I asked for something that was in alignment with God's will, that did not mean 1) it would happen in my timing or 2) it was going to be the answer I had in my mind, or even really understood, at the time. And just because He reveals the next part of His will for my life, and perhaps even gives me a vision of the end result, that does not mean I'm able to see His full master plan or that He'll reveal all the choices, hard or otherwise, I'll have to make on the way there. And most importantly, when He tells me to sit still while I wait for what He's promised me, my obedience is critical.

Why, Lord?

Remember that fog I talked about in the chapter on "The Wait" and how there is a reason for it? I've come to learn that it is there to protect us from our own limited understanding of the Big Picture. God's will for our lives unfolds in stages, I believe, because it requires us to trust Him along the way. It allows us to build belief, wisdom, and patience, all virtues He wants us to have. That's what faith is all about.

It sure is difficult sometimes though, isn't it? Sometimes I find myself like Habakkuk, shaking my head and asking constantly: why, Lord? I'm doing all the right things (well most of them, most of the time anyway), living as righteous a life as I can in this fallen world, and yet, I just don't understand why you're letting or not letting certain things happen for me.

> Commit everything you do to the Lord. Trust him, and he will help you. . . . Be still in the presence of the Lord and wait patiently for him to act . . .
>
> —Psalm 37:5, 7a (NLT)

You know what Habakkuk had to do after He asked God all of the tough questions about why He was letting certain things happen that just didn't seem fair or right? He had to sit still and listen. In the end God revealed to him that He had a bigger plan in place, and while it may not have looked like things were happening in the favor of the righteous in the moment, God would bring about all He promised them. And then Habakkuk trusted and waited. (Note: When you're struggling with tough questions for God, read the book of Habakkuk. It's only three chapters, and even though it's from the Old Testament, there's some good, relevant insight in there for today's world.)

If you are someone like me who's constantly lived her life making the statement "I can't wait until . . .", you will struggle with this concept. I still do from time to time. When I do, I remind myself of where the abundant life exists, and the fact that even though I may not have exactly what He's promised me yet, there's some pretty amazing things happening in the right now . . . if I'm tuned in to it.

Trusting Him

> Blessed is she who has believed that the Lord would fulfill his promises to her!
>
> —Luke 1:45 (NIV)

I wonder sometimes why it's so hard to trust in the one person who's overqualified to keep promises, the one who cannot fail, the one who is not even capable of making a mistake. Is it because we can't physically see Him? Is it because we relate to Him like any other person we've trusted to keep their promises and failed in their human attempts? I'm not sure. One thing I am sure of—everyone who has put their trust in the Lord and faithfully obeyed His command got what He promised them. Noah, Hannah, Joseph, and Job, just to name a few. And even some who weren't so obedient or faithful at times—Abraham and Sarah, David, and Solomon—all received promises made to them by God.

Perhaps we've convinced ourselves that our way to get to what He's promised us is better than His way because we haven't gone all in with our belief that He will do it. We believe it's in our own power to make His promise happen. That's what the world wants us to believe, anyway.

Maybe we don't trust sometimes because He doesn't fulfill His promises in the way or timing we hoped. I believe that's the struggle for most of us; at least it has been for me. At times I've felt like I needed to help God along. It's as if I'm saying, "Hey God, remember me and my situation? If I just get things in motion, maybe you'll take it from there."

But God doesn't work like that. God doesn't need us to help Him along. He doesn't take our lead. We're designed to take His lead. And that level of trust, for Him to lead, requires a level of spiritual maturity that most will never acquire. It's the same reason most people who attempt entrepreneurship will fail, and why most people will not become physically fit or become wealthy. It takes sacrifice, commitment, patience, discipline, obedience, perseverance, tenacity—a whole host of characteristics and virtues that are not for the faint of heart.

I don't want to paint a picture here that everyone is doomed to fail, because I believe quite the contrary. The good news is that God wired us for faith and all those other attributes. He designed us, in all of our intricacies, to praise Him and worship Him and, yes, trust Him. We just have to find our way back to that innate ability. Culture, society, and the world and its false idols have steered us away, but we can find our way back.

We do have the ability; the challenge is the choice. We must choose Him daily. No matter how strong or weak our faith is, we have to choose to trust and have faith in Him and His promises every day. It's not a one-time decision. You make the decision once and you are saved, but you have to choose daily to trust Him and be obedient to His will. You have to make choices every day to be patient and trust that God is working things out for your good, even when you don't see evidence of that promise . . . *yet*.

Let us hold on firmly to the hope we profess, because we can trust God to keep his promise.

—Hebrews 10:23 (GNT)

REFLECTIONS

REFLECTIONS

God's Delays Are Not Always His Denials

Journal Entry (December 30, 2015)

I'm sitting here on our balcony in Dubai, our home for the next seven days, feeling extremely grateful. I've wanted to come here for a long time, and now I'm here. It's beautiful. The sun is shining, the water is blue and glistening, there's not a cloud to be found in the sky . . . A part of me is thinking, had I gotten what I thought I wanted a few years ago as far as my life and the direction of it was concerned, I wouldn't have had the chance to experience this.

As I look at my Facebook timeline flooded with engagement and baby announcements, sometimes I have to admit it has made me feel a bit inadequate and disappointed that those things haven't happened for me yet. But as I gained some perspective (at least for today ☺), I realize I'm right where I should be for the moment. Those things are coming, and I don't have to rush it, or be anxious or feel any of those feelings that, honestly, are from the enemy. When I see it for what it is, I realize it's only the enemy trying to steal my joy. I feel good now when I can distinguish the enemy's tricks faster and disregard them as lies. The truth is, I am blessed to be right here in this moment. I have so many things for which to be grateful.

I do need to think about and really pray on what God wants me to do and accomplish in 2016. But I can't force or rush that either. I just need to be (and stay) in tune with Him. I need to trust in my ability to hear His voice and be obedient when He calls.

God's Delays

We've probably heard "hindsight is always 20/20" a thousand times. While cliché, it is true. We can always look back on a situation and say, with 100 percent clarity, "oh, that's why that happened," or "man, if I had just waited, I would have gotten this," or how about, "had I known then what I know now, I would have made a different choice."

Truth is, God is our hindsight. He has better than 20/20 vision, because it's His plan. He knows what's going to happen even before it happens. He's already factored every single choice we could make into each scenario and woven them together.

Once I really understood this concept, which was quite recent, I started to have another perspective on God's "delays." I put His delays in quotes because they are only a delay to us. To Him it is on time. As James Banks put it in his *Our Daily Bread* devotion from November 6, 2017, "God's timing is rarely our own, but it is always worth waiting for."

So now, when I think about something that I want really badly, I remind myself that there is a reason for this timing, *His* timing. Perhaps I need to learn something while I wait. Perhaps the other person or people involved are not ready. Maybe God has something for me to accomplish or pursue while I wait on this thing. Or, what if this delay is giving me time to rethink if this is something I truly desire?

God's Blessings

As I look back on some of those times of delay in my life, I realize they have actually been blessings. I can honestly say that during those seasons, I learned more and grew more spiritually than I did during any season of contentment. Additionally, who knows from what some of those delays saved me?

During that nearly five-year relationship that I thought would result in marriage, I often asked God why it hadn't happened yet. Looking back with fresh eyes and a newfound perspective from hindsight, the delay was there for my own good. I was in love, we had built a bond, and I thought it was "my time," so I ignored some pretty obvious red flags that were staring me in the face. Had I gotten my way and we had married, we would have dealt with some serious and no doubt painful issues within our marriage that likely would have broken and ended us before we had a chance to start.

What I could not see was the bigger picture I talked about in my first chapter. Had I plowed full speed ahead with my plans and my timing and not really stopped to take time to ask God for discernment, to be still and consult Him on what to do next, I really could have caused myself some unnecessary heartache. And don't be mistaken, in the past I've done that too, and suffered the consequences.

We have to remember that God has a plan for us and it is good. In fact, it is better than good. When He brings about any type of delay on something we really desire, we have to stop and consider how it could be part of His larger plan, rather than trying to figure out how we can plow our way through to the other side as fast as we can.

The Lord works out everything to its proper end.

—Proverbs 16:4a (NIV)

God's Denials

While we're on the subject, we do need to consider that sometimes there will be denials. Sometimes God gives us the delay on the way to the denial to prepare our hearts for not getting what we want. I believe that was the case in that nearly five-year relationship. That delay was meaningful. Over time, I saw how that relationship was not God's best for me. Time and space to look back and see that relationship for what it was gave me a newfound perspective that I would not have gained had I stuck in there, or worse, plowed through to make it happen. Now, it still hurt like hell and it took me nearly a year to recover, but I can't even imagine the type of pain I would have felt had I moved forward anyway, found myself in a miserable marriage, and had to go through the heartbreak of divorce.

I can also think about some job opportunities and clients I wanted to work with that turned out to be denials. At the time of learning that I had not been accepted to work on those projects, I felt rejected. I wrestled with questions like, "am I good enough?" and "am I cut out for this?", and it definitely took some wind out of my sails. Then, when I really began to get close to God and ask Him the tough questions I had a hard time answering myself, He revealed that He provided those denials for a reason.

In some cases, I learned later that a couple of those jobs I wanted were with companies that were soon to go out of business unexpectedly, and some of those potential clients would not have been able to sustain their work with me. In other cases, it turned out there was nothing wrong with those opportunities, God just had something better around the corner. What an amazing God!

God's Track Record

If you've learned anything from this book, I hope you've gotten that God can and should be trusted. He is the epitome of integrity.

> Then Jesus said to the disciples, "Have faith in God. I tell you the truth, you can say to this mountain, 'May you be lifted up and thrown into the sea,' and it will happen. But you must really believe it will happen and have no doubt in your heart. I tell you, you can pray for anything, and if you believe that you've received it, it will be yours."
>
> —Mark 11:22–24 (NLT)

When we truly believe in and trust that God will do what He has promised, amazing things happen. While God does most of the heavy lifting, it does require work on our part—the work of believing and trusting. For some of us, that is really hard to do. We've been hurt, betrayed, and disappointed, beaten up by life (and perhaps even by the church) so much that we have a hard time trusting anyone, including God. But please know, His track record is good, impeccable in fact. And we don't have to look too hard for evidence of that.

Even if you've had what you would consider a hard life, I'm sure you can think of numerous occasions where God has shown up and turned things around that seemed nearly impossible, where He showed you grace and mercy instead of letting you suffer the hard consequences of your mistakes and sins, and where He healed you from suffering and pain that at the time you thought would never end.

I know I'm not the only one who suffers from selective memory at times. When I feel disappointment creeping up and I start to complain about what I don't have right now or what I've lost, I have to remind myself of God's track record in my life. How He's blessed me over and over again, even in the midst of my trials, delays, and denials. Even when I can't see why He lets certain things happen, I know it's ultimately for my good.

> And we know that God causes everything to work together for the good of those who love God and are called according to his purpose for them.
>
> —Romans 8:28 (NLT)

I know, trust me, the hard part many times is trying not to confuse our definition or understanding of what "good" looks like with what His is. "Wait a minute God, I thought you said all things would work together for my good. Why am I experiencing hardship?"

Let's go back to the story of Job for a minute. Job had been blessed tremendously with a wife and children, a thriving business, and, I'm sure, all of the trappings that come along with living a wealthy life. Then the unthinkable happened. Every single one of Job's children passed away, he lost his home and his business, and on top of that, a major illness brought him physical pain and suffering. After his wife, who also had experienced heartbreak and loss, told him that he needed to "curse God and die," his response to her was "shall we accept good from God, and not trouble?" (Job 2:9–10 NIV)

Don't get me wrong. Job had some really tough moments. At one point, he even questioned why he had been born and asked God to take his life. But he understood that the time we spend here on Earth is not always about us getting what we want, and that just because we experience hardship, it does not mean God is punishing us or not working out His good plan for us. Job's good plan included his hardship and struggle.

The end of his story reveals that he was given twice as much as he had before and his latter days were blessed more than his beginning. The struggle and the hardship all served a purpose. And in the end, God's track record remained intact, just as it always does.

The Lord guides us in the way we should go and protects those who please him. If they fall, they will not stay down, because the Lord will help them up.

Psalm 37:23–24 (GNT)

REFLECTIONS

REFLECTIONS

Forgiveness

Journal Entry (January 11, 2016)

I spoke to God this morning and He revealed something to me that I believe will be the catalyst for my answered prayer as it relates to my sleeping Adam: I needed to forgive myself. Even though in my previous journal entries I talked about how I played my own role in the incidences with men last year, I never had the epiphany that I needed to forgive myself. I've forgiven them for their role, even the one who didn't apologize, but I failed to forgive the most important person in this equation—the one I have to live with every day—myself.

I've wanted so badly to completely let all of this stuff I've been holding onto go. I was still holding onto a few things, but this was the missing piece to letting them all go: forgive myself and then move on. Thank you, Father, for that revelation. Amen.

Don't Hurt Yourself

Most of the time when people talk about forgiveness, it is in the context of forgiving another person. Speaking for myself, I have oftentimes been so focused on the hurt and disappointments that others have caused in my life, I forget about the hurtful self-talk and guilt trips I have with myself that can be just as detrimental to my progress. For a perfectionist like me who tends to beat herself up a lot, this was an important revelation.

Forgiveness is a powerful action, particularly when the recipient of that forgiveness is your own self. Unless I'm some type of unicorn and I'm the only one who operates this way, I would venture to say that most of us as humans do not think about the pain, hurt, and disappointment we've inflicted on ourselves by constantly reflecting within and not giving ourselves a break. Some of us don't even look within, because we're so busy blaming others for our hurt. But when you do look within and take ownership of the responsibility you had in the matter that hurt you, how many times have you gone through the process of actually saying "I forgive you" to yourself? Until this journal entry, it was a thought I had not really considered.

> Repent, then, and turn to God, so that your sins may be wiped out, that times of refreshing may come from the Lord.
>
> —Acts 3:19 (NIV)

How often have we hindered our own growth and progress by not offering ourselves the same grace God offers us? Once I found the power of forgiving myself, it gave me so much peace. My soul was refreshed, as the scripture states. Conversely, if we hold onto the guilt, the suffering that comes along with not forgiving ourselves for the wrongs we've done to ourselves and others, we become crippled and remain broken. And unfortunately, that's how we end up hurting others and ourselves even more. I'm sure you've heard the statement: "Hurt people hurt people." It's a fact. The sooner we can forgive ourselves, the sooner we can begin to heal ourselves and break the cycle.

Take Responsibility

The other way we can stop hurting ourselves is to start accepting responsibility for our own healing when someone else hurts us. Many of us are wallowing in pain that someone else inflicted on us months, years, even decades ago. Our excuse for holding onto it is simply that we just can't let it go. We make statements like, "Well, I'm just a person who holds grudges." or "There's no way I can forgive and forget." We have to understand that when we take that stance, ultimately the only person we're hurting is ourselves.

> But when you are praying, first forgive anyone you are holding a grudge against, so that your Father in heaven will forgive your sins, too.
>
> —Mark 11:25 (NLT)

God created us in His image. We are His image bearers. Therefore, as God is a forgiving God, we certainly have the capacity to forgive others as well. The question is not whether we are capable of forgiving, rather, if we *will* forgive. To rest on the idea that God made you that way, made you someone who holds grudges and doesn't forgive, is simply false and lazy. Hear me out before you shut the book and stop reading. Forgiveness is hard work. It takes a level of maturity, strength, and humility to forgive someone when they've done something to hurt us, even more so when they've done something to hurt us multiple times.

> If we confess our sins, he is faithful and just and will forgive us our sins and purify us from all unrighteousness.
>
> —1 John 1:9 (NIV)

Jesus said if there were one commandment that trumps all the others, it would be to love God with all of our hearts; and the second one, right behind it, would be to love others. Do you know what God's definition and instructions on love are? Paul gave the supreme definition of love and what it means to love others, imparted from God, in 1 Corinthians 13:4–8. I know that any of us who have ever been to a wedding are familiar with these verses. We have just chosen to ignore the part that says that love means keeping no record of being wronged. That's forgiveness on a whole other level! And yes, forgiveness is wrapped up in one of the greatest commandments, which is to love others.

Love is patient and kind. Love is not jealous or boastful or proud or rude. It does not demand its own way. It is not irritable, and it keeps no record of being wronged. It does not rejoice about injustice but rejoices whenever the truth wins out. Love never gives up, never loses faith, is always hopeful, and endures through every circumstance. Prophecy and speaking in unknown languages and special knowledge will become useless. But love will last forever!

1 Corinthians 13:4–8 (NLT)

REFLECTIONS

REFLECTIONS

My Sleeping Adam

This notion of my "Sleeping Adam" has been on my heart since I first heard the words spoken at a women's conference I was working at in Atlanta in July 2015. It was the same year I was healing from one of the most painful breakups of my life. I had convinced myself I was going to marry a man that God did not call to be my husband. I wanted it to be true because I loved him and I had invested so much time, energy, and love, and so much of myself, into the relationship. But I was disobedient from the beginning. I ignored the red flags. I ignored our initial conversation about him not being ready to be in a relationship because of where he was in his life. I ignored him and I ignored God's whispers.

So, when I heard Dr. Wanda Davis Turner explain this concept of a Sleeping Adam, a light bulb went off for me. Adam was asleep when God performed the surgery on him to bring Eve to life. God had already done most of the work on Adam before the surgery, but the final part of the process was his induced coma for God to prepare Eve for him.

And there was the epiphany: Some of us as women are trying to wake men up who are still "sleeping." That time of sleep is a preparation time for him while God is putting the finishing touches on who he is as a man and, ultimately, as a husband. We fail to realize that God put him to sleep for a reason. If we wake him up before he's ready, we stand the chance of getting a mate who is half asleep or not complete on his own, meaning he needs someone else to make him complete. I think most, if not all, women have experienced or at least seen the consequences of that.

That "Sleeping Adam" term spoke to my heart so profoundly, I started using it in my journal entries. What she said made so much sense, and it explained many of the struggles I had in my dating experiences. The men I wanted, or thought I wanted, were still sleeping, and I was trying to wake them up. I was trying so hard to get them to see the value in me, not realizing that that was never really the issue.

Most of my adult life I've been with both half-asleep and half-complete men. The reason I felt like I had to lead them was because they weren't ready to lead, and there was nothing I could do to make them be ready. I heard many times, "when a man is ready, he is ready." And you can't *make* him ready before that time. For those women who do manage to wake their Sleeping Adams up before their process is complete, and cajole them into a marriage via an ultimatum, they ultimately end up regretting it in the long run.

I needed to go through those experiences to learn the lesson: If Adam is not coming for Eve, it doesn't mean Eve is not amazing or that Adam doesn't see her value. It might mean he's still asleep. If that is the case, you have a decision to make. Wait for him to wake up (if you believe he's worth waiting for) or move on, but please don't try to wake him up before he's finished sleeping!

I'm not one of those people who believes in soul mates in the sense that there is just one person on this Earth for everyone. But I do believe God has placed His best for us strategically in our lives for us to choose. There are many scenarios that will work based on the myriad decisions we make. That's why there's no mistake we can make that God hasn't already factored into His plan. The book has already been written. The course has already been set. I've learned His best plans come when we act according to His will and His timing. And we could always save ourselves a lot of pain, suffering, and time by just being obedient and patient.

REFLECTIONS

REFLECTIONS

Conclusion

I want you to know that I wrote this book with you in mind. I shared some of the most intimate parts of myself with you, not just to save you from making some of the mistakes I did (though I do hope that is one of the byproducts as well), but also to share with you that you are not alone in making them. I want you to know that you don't have to beat yourself up for them. Your mistakes can be useful to you, just as mine have been purposeful for me. And sometimes life's events that really throw us for a loop are not of our doing at all; rather, they were ordained by God to accomplish His overall purpose.

This doesn't give us a permission slip to live life recklessly, because at the end of the day, we are all responsible for our actions. We will be held accountable for them. But bad things and less than desirable situations are going to happen to us all—good people and bad. God wants us to know, however, that our best lives—our most rich and fulfilling, abundant lives—are lived by getting close to Him and honoring Him with our obedience. He's got the roadmap; we've just got to follow it. When we do, we won't have to wait for the hereafter to experience His goodness, we'll get to have it right now in this world, which we have a hand in making a better place.

> I would have lost heart, unless I had believed that I would see the goodness of the Lord in the land of the living. Wait on the Lord; be of good courage, and he shall strengthen your heart; Wait, I say, on the Lord!
>
> —Psalm 27:13–14 (NKJV)

REFLECTIONS

REFLECTIONS

References

Baker Publishing Group, comp. *Moments of Peace in the Presence of God: Morning and Evening Edition*. Bloomington, Minnesota: Bethany House Publishers, 2010.

Banks, James. "Our Prayers, God's Timing." *Our Daily Bread*. November 6, 2017. https://odb.org/2017/11/06/our-prayers-gods-timing.

Roberts, Touré. *Purpose Awakening: Discover the Epic Idea that Motivated Your Birth*. New York: FaithWords, 2014.

Scriptures marked CSB are taken from The Christian Standard Bible. Copyright © 2017 by Holman Bible Publishers. Used by permission. Christian Standard Bible®, and CSB® are federally registered trademarks of Holman Bible Publishers, all rights reserved.

Scriptures marked ESV are taken from English Standard Version®. Copyright © 2001 by Crossway, a publishing ministry of Good News Publishers. All rights reserved.

Scriptures marked GNT are taken from the Good News Translation® — Second Edition. Copyright © 1992 by American Bible Society. All rights reserved.

Scriptures marked MSG are taken from The Message®. Copyright © 1993, 1994, 1995, 1996, 2000, 2001, 2002. Used by permission of NavPress Publishing Group.

Scriptures marked NIV are taken from the New International Version®. Copyright © 1973, 1978, 1984, 2011 by Biblica, Inc.™. All rights reserved.

Scriptures marked NKJV are taken from the New King James Version®. Copyright © 1982 by Thomas Nelson. All rights reserved.

Scriptures marked NLT are taken from the New Living Translation®. Copyright © 1996, 2004, 2007, 2013 by Tyndale House Foundation. All rights reserved.

About the Author

An entrepreneur of nearly fifteen years, Leslie Green is a communications professional and the founder and CEO of Golden Life Ventures, LLC, a travel and lifestyle company. She also recently launched a new division, Golden Life Ministries, where she speaks and writes about the Christian faith. Her first love is music and entertainment, and she currently serves as the creative director, as well as singer and songwriter for Greenhouse Entertainment, her family-run music production company.

Leslie is committed to living life boldly and to the fullest—what she calls the golden life—and desires to help others experience a golden and abundant life. She is an active member of her church, Zion Church, where she serves on several ministries, and volunteers at Calvary Women's Services, a transitional home for homeless women. Her hobbies include cooking, dancing, and listening to live music. Leslie lives in Washington, DC.

To learn more, visit her website at www.goldenlifeventures.com

CREATING DISTINCTIVE BOOKS
WITH INTENTIONAL RESULTS

We're a collaborative group of creative masterminds with a mission to produce high-quality books to position you for monumental success in the marketplace.

Our professional team of writers, editors, designers, and marketing strategists work closely together to ensure that every detail of your book is a clear representation of the message in your writing.

Want to know more?
Write to us at info@publishyourgift.com
or call (888) 949-6228

Discover great books, exclusive offers, and more at
www.PublishYourGift.com

Connect with us on social media

@publishyourgift

www.ingramcontent.com/pod-product-compliance
Lightning Source LLC
Chambersburg PA
CBHW052141110526
44591CB00012B/1817